The Running Experience

The Running Experience

BILL DELLINGER
BLAINE NEWNHAM
WARREN MORGAN

Library of Congress Cataloging in Publication Data

Dellinger, Bill.
The running experience.

Includes index.
1. Jogging. 2. Running. I. Newnham, Blaine, joint author. II. Morgan, Warren, joint author. III. Title.
GV494.D44 1978 796.4'26 78-57472
ISBN 0-8092-7519-8
ISBN 0-8092-7517-1 pbk.

All photos by Warren Morgan unless noted.

Published by Contemporary Books, Inc.
180 North Michigan Avenue, Chicago, Illinois 60601
Manufactured in the United States of America
Library of Congress Catalog Card Number: 78-57472
International Standard Book Number: 0-8092-7519-8 (cloth)
0-8092-7517-1 (paper)

Published simultaneously in Canada by
Beaverbooks
953 Dillingham Road
Pickering, Ontario L1W 1Z7
Canada

Contents

Preface

Like many who wondered if a worthwhile fad might ever follow hula hoops, goldfish swallowing, and the stuffing of telephone booths, we are in awe of the current craze to run and jog, as well as the more lofty goal of physical fitness. The *New York Times*, marveling at the turnout of over 5,000 for the 1977 New York Marathon, estimated that 15 million Americans have taken to running. Another source put the number at more than 11 million Americans now running regularly, up from 3.5 million in 1975 and a mere 100,000 or so in 1968.

We are in awe but would be less than honest if we didn't also admit to a certain smugness. Yes, an I-told-you-so attitude. For more than 15 years now, jogging has been as much a part of the Oregon countryside as rain, fresh air, and tall trees. Many of our joggers have run daily for better than half their lives. Eugene, Oregon, isn't famous for a big race—there is no equivalent to the Boston Marathon or San Francisco's Bay-to-Breakers—but for its everyday runners who slip easily through a morning mist to their appointed rounds of two, three, four, or five miles each day. More than 10,000 of Eugene's 100,000 people are devoted to running, and have come to understand the principles Bill Bowerman first used in making the University of Oregon home for America's four-minute milers.

If one were to seek the roots of the American jogger he would find them in Eugene. The city has showcased international track meets, but its real fame lies in a population that runs for the love of running.

Bill Bowerman, my coach and for many years the coach at the University of Oregon, brought the jogging message to Eugene in 1962 from New Zealand. He wrote a book, *Jogging,* that sold more than a million copies. The man who helped him write that first book, Jim Shea, left Eugene in 1970 to become a vice president of Temple University in Philadelphia. Jim missed Eugene and its environment and on January 14, 1970, wrote me this letter:

"There's a respectability about track at Oregon that I've never seen anyplace else. Track is not looked on as a sport, but more as 'a good thing to do.' Even that obstreperous bunch, the faculty, support track and never sniped at it. The whole state turns out for meets. Kids run, grandmas jog, and pregnant women waddle, and no one looks up from the evening paper as they go by, because running and jogging in Oregon are part of the setting, like the fir trees. I've tried to figure out what it is that Oregon has that lets superstars perform as superstars and turns the average kid into a good runner. Oregon's got great weather; never too hot or cold to train outdoors. It's got great facilities; including the natural kind for relaxed cross-country training. It's got an appreciative populace who regard runners only slightly behind the Oregon pioneers."

For a runner, there is no place like Oregon. Early the attention was focused on runners such as Jim Bailey, Dyrol Burleson, Jim Grelle, Kenny Moore, and the late Steve ("Pre") Prefontaine. The shrine was Hayward Field, the track stadium which hosted the last two United States

Olympic trials in track and field as well as other national meets, and was the site of many of Pre's greatest races.

But we too have felt a change in emphasis. More people are participating, less likely satisfied to be just a spectator. The new mecca for runners is Pre's Trail, nearly five miles of soft trails winding through a park in the heart of the city. Runners, many of them just ambling joggers, come to Eugene to run the facility dedicated in 1975 to the great and charismatic runner whose life was snuffed out by a tragic automobile accident.

Pre would wave to joggers as he passed them on his daily run through the South Eugene hills. He taught a jogging class for the Eugene recreation department, and had worked for the jogging facility that bears his name long before his death.

Jogging is not a fad in Eugene. Physical fitness is important to our joggers, but the zealots have long ago wandered away to find a new fad. We're hopeful that the dreams and devotions of our runners will be both inspirational and helpful to you; that the enduring jogging experience of Eugene can be your jogging experience; and that the training schedules and principles I have used in coaching Steve Prefontaine will be the aid to you I think they can be.

1

In the Beginning

It was a Sunday afternoon in the spring of 1962. John Kennedy was president, the country was beginning to awake from the intellectual hibernation of the 1950s, and Bill Bowerman was inspired to get Americans on their feet. He jogged down to the track at the University of Oregon that day and could not believe what he was seeing. Nearly a thousand residents of Eugene, Oregon (50,000-population), were there to help Bowerman kick off his jogging program. Another town might have been stuffing telephone booths. Or Volkswagens. A month earlier he had begun with a first group of 25 interested in jogging. Nearly 50 came as interest grew. But on the fourth weekend of his grand experiment, word had spread across town that *Life* magazine would be on hand to photograph Eugene's joggers, as would the local television stations and newspapers.

"There were fat old women, fat old men, and one guy ran by me looking as if he might have a stroke right there," recalled Bowerman, then a man of 50 and perhaps America's most famous track and field coach. "So I just said 'Hey, let's wait a minute. I don't want to be responsible for somebody having a serious problem.'" And Bowerman sent them all home.

And jogging had begun in America. In the weeks that followed, Bowerman and a Eugene cardiologist, Dr. Waldo Harris, put together a jogging program for Americans of any age and almost any state of fitness. Harris drew upon his research in cardiology, and Bowerman on his keen knowledge of distance running. Both were impressed with the fitness of Oregon's heralded sub-four-minute milers. Jim Bailey, an Australian who ran for Bill at the University of Oregon, ran the first sub-four-minute mile on American soil. I was to set numerous American records under Bowerman and run in three Olympic Games, climaxed by my winning a bronze medal in the Tokyo Olympics. Bowerman's teams at Oregon won four national collegiate track championships, but it was his distance runners who drew the most attention: Jim Bailey, Bill Dellinger, Dyrol Burleson, Jim Grelle, Archie San Ramoni, Roscoe Divine, Kenny Moore, and, of course, the late Steve Prefontaine.

"But," said Bowerman one day recently from his home in the hills overlooking the town he helped make famous, "if I did anything for my community and my state it was the small part I played in helping to get people jogging." Retired from coaching at the University of Oregon in 1973 when I succeeded him as coach, Bill still works as a vice president in charge of research for the Nike Shoe Company of Beaverton, Oregon. "My knee goes to sleep when I jog anymore," he says, "so I walk." And he does, religiously and regularly.

Bowerman's early interest in jogging was concentrated almost entirely in Eugene. In the three years that followed his first development of a jogging program with Dr. Harris, over 1,000 people in the community went through closely supervised programs. There were isolated cases across the country of people running for fun and physical fitness at a slow pace, but no such community-wide assault on fat and inactivity as was going on in Eugene. Finally, in 1966 Bowerman and Harris—tired of answering mail about their new approach to fitness and anxious to spread the word—put out a 20-page pamphlet "Jogging." "We sold it for 35 cents a copy, and at that were less than breaking even," said Bowerman. "When we were each $1,000 in the hole we realized we had to stop this nonsense—the price of spreading the gospel had become too high." Bowerman and Harris hooked up with a New York publisher, Grosset and Dunlap, and the next year, 1967, came forth with an expanded 127-page book which was to sell over a million copies and be printed in Japanese and Dutch as well as English. All current books on running relate back to the original Bowerman book and his coaching principles, which have developed the hard-easy training method, the talk test, and the undying principle of training: Don't strain. Bowerman and Harris successfully extracted the basic elements of a program which trained gifted athletes to run the mile in less than four minutes and applied them to the average person and his quest for physical fitness.

In the winter of 1962, shortly after the University of Oregon's four-mile relay team had broken the world record, an invitation came for a match race with the New Zealand team which had previously held the record. Bowerman and his runners were the guests of Arthur Lydiard, the New Zealand Olympic coach. Although both Bowerman and Lydiard were celebrated internationally as successful distance running coaches, Lydiard had long been at work developing jogging programs, beginning with some of his runners who were about to retire from competition and who were unwilling to give up the high level of fitness built through training. Lydiard came up with the idea of combining conditioning with the stimulus of companionship by slow, steady cross-country running done in loosely organized groups, or jogging clubs.

"The first Sunday I was down there," said Bowerman, "Lydiard asked me if I wanted to go out for a run with a local jogging club. I was used to going out and walking 55

Bill Bowerman returned to his native Oregon and took his runners on the long, steady jogs he had experienced in New Zealand. (Photo by Joe Matheson)

yards, jogging 55 yards, go about a quarter of a mile and figure that I had done quite a bit. Lydiard was late picking me up, so I thought, 'What the hell, I'll get some breakfast.' I was eating a big bowl of Oatmeal in the dining room when here comes Lydiard. So we go out and meet a couple of hundred people in a park—men, women, children, all ages, and all sizes. I was still full of breakfast as Lydiard pointed toward a hill in the distance and said we were going to run to Two Pine Knoll. It looked about a mile-and-a-half away. We took off and I wasn't too bad for about a half-mile, and then we started up this hill. God, the only thing that kept me alive was the hope that I would die. I moved right to the back of the group and an old fellow, I suppose he was around 70 years old, moved back with me and said, 'I see you're having trouble.' I didn't say anything . . . because I couldn't. Then he said, 'I know a shortcut.' So we took off down the hill and got back about the same time the people did who covered the whole distance.

"I had a number of traumatic experiences after that," continued Bowerman, who was then 50 years old, slightly overweight, but in what he thought was reasonably good condition. And if he weren't in as good shape as someone, he could certainly be a tougher competitor than they were. Bowerman had been a rough and tumble high school and college football player, and was noted for his zeal on the track.

"It was after another coaching clinic that I decided to run again," he said. "There were a couple of gals, about 30 I guess, running and I said to myself, 'I'll stay somewhere near those gals.' We approached a hill and I knew they'd slow up. But, if anything, they went faster up the hill. I saw Lydiard afterwards and said, 'I don't mind your 70-year-old men and your kids showing me how physically unfit I am, but those two girls running me in the ground . . . that does it.' Lydiard laughed like hell, and told me that one of them was the New Zealand women's 800-meter record-holder. Which didn't encourage me a great deal."

Bowerman spent six weeks in New Zealand and began running every day. He lost between five and ten pounds, but, more importantly, reduced his waist by four inches. Nearing the end of his stay, he and Lydiard went on a sight-seeing tour of the South Island. Lydiard coaxed Bowerman on a jog to an abandoned ghost town. "He told me it was five miles," said Bowerman, "but we'd run only a few hundred yards and came to a sign which said 12 miles. But we went at my pace—a slow, comfortable jog—crossed a creek a few times running up this canyon, and sooner than I thought, and without any of the distress I thought I'd have, we were there. It had taken up almost two hours to get there." Bowerman had learned how to jog. Upon his return to Eugene, he was anxious to keep jogging himself and to tell others about his own success and that which he had seen among the jogging clubs and people of New Zealand.

No sooner had he arrived home than Bowerman received a phone call from Jerry Uhrhammer, a sports writer for the *Eugene Register-Guard.* "He wanted to know how our team had performed, and if I'd learned anything about running," Bowerman recalled. "I told him the competition was great, but that the biggest thing that happened to me down there was that I had learned my idea of exercise was way low. 'Those people down there,' I said, 'thousands of them jog. Their women jog, their kids jog, everybody jogs.' And he said to me, 'Do you think we could do it here?' "

So Uhrhammer, who was later to take up jogging after undergoing open-heart surgery to save his life, published a few articles about Bowerman's discovery. A couple dozen came out for Bowerman's first joggers' meeting, then 50, then 75 and then the decisive crowd of 1,000 after Uhrhammer had written of possible national exposure for Eugene's unique group of joggers. It was at that point that Bowerman sought the medical expertise of Harris. The two met three or four times until Harris understood Bowerman's understanding of exercise, and Harris finally said, "Let's take your running program for a four-minute

"If I did anything for Eugene and Oregon," reflected Bill Bowerman, "it was the small part I played in helping to get people jogging."

miler and cut it back 90 percent. What do you think of that?" Bowerman, who was excited about the idea of making his distance running program available to all, said, "You're the doctor." So the two wrote a program based on an interval of 25 seconds for 110 yards—or slightly more than a brisk walk.

"We started out with the idea that they would do intervals until they could handle a continuous jog," said Bowerman. Four university faculty members were a part of the first three-month gradually progressive program. Harris administered physical examinations to all those in the program and monitored their progress very closely. After the first four had finished the pilot program, Bowerman and Harris went to the local YMCA and started with a larger group of 100 joggers, split into 10 groups with 10 of Oregon's best distance runners doing the coaching. "We checked weight loss," said Bowerman, "and it was dramatic among the overweight. There was a better feeling of well-being among the joggers. In fact, almost without exception they began to feel more tigerish."

In the preface to his original book, Bowerman wrote: "Jogging is a graduated program of moderate exercise which can be adapted to men and women of varying ages and levels of fitness. Jogging is a simple type of exercise, requiring no highly developed skills. Its great appeal is that it is so handy. Almost anyone can do it anywhere. Our concern is to keep it simple, not let it become hidden in some mystique full of rules and paraphernalia."

And although Bowerman was a fierce competitor as an athlete and a coach, and although his runners were among the world's best, he understood jogging's place for the average American. In fact, his definition of jogging called it "a kind of running, generally a slow regular trot that has been described as the next step up from walking."

It was a long way from the world of four-milers and the keen and uncompromising sense of competition Bowerman had known as a runner himself. But it was a way for him, approaching senior citizenship, to hold and perpetuate the

Bowerman and his wife take a brisk walk over Pre's Trail, still practicing what Bowerman preached 15 years earlier.

values of physical fitness. And for Americans of all ages and nearly all stages of physical fitness to run away from society's unknowing conspiracy for a sedentary life.

Bowerman planted his seeds in fertile ground. His track teams had made a community aware of runners. In the mild, Northwest winters, people were yearning for an activity that could reasonably take place in a light winter rain. Oregonians are a free, independent sort who cherish their countryside and relish time in the outdoors. So jogging had arrived from New Zealand. And the little town in Oregon would never be the same again.

2

The Reason We Run

At the University of Oregon and throughout the community, for that matter, we've always talked about running in the same breath with brushing your teeth. I guess Bill Bowerman said it first. But Kenny Moore repeats it, and Jon Anderson tells it to people everywhere; it's just the way we feel about our avocation. Those who pound the pavement grow to feel the same way.

"Jogging is likc brushing your teeth; don't do it for three or four days and you just won't feel right."

We can talk a lot about the reasons why we jog, but most people start exercising out of fear. It's not that they want to feel better, look sharper, and live longer. Rather, they don't want to get any worse than they already are. Unfortunately, the motivation is often negative, not positive. Too many of us start out repenting for other failures. Physical activity can actually be masochistic for those who find themselves paying the price for indulgence. You know it won't be fun, but what in life is worthwhile without sacrifice and pain? Right? Remember your mother telling you that the medicine couldn't possibly do you any good unless it stung? Traditionally, we have all been told that exercise isn't accomplished—and productive—without pain.

And, too, running has often been the price we paid for failure or mistakes. Football players still run stadium steps for being late to practice, overweight men run because they eat too much, and the Army makes its recruits run a mile in a specified time or flunk a physical fitness test. Maybe that Army mile is the only mile you've ever run. Perhaps you ran penalty wind sprints. And now you're thinking about running again, this time because you're overweight, or because good physical condition is quickly and obviously slipping away. Or at least over your belt.

You may start jogging for those reasons, but we're willing to bet that the jogger who is still putting in his roadwork a year from when he reads this will cite the emotional and psychological benefits of running to those who will listen, and it was long ago that he was concerned about his heart and lungs.

And, yet, there seems to be no question that some form of consistent physical exercise will improve our general state of fitness. Exercise that is strenuous enough to significantly increase the heart rate will increase the strength of the heart as it pumps both slower and more efficiently. Literally more ounces of blood are pushed through the body with less effort. A general improvement of the cardiovascular system will follow. Dr. T.J. Bassler says simply: "Life expectancy is proportional to the distance you can cover on foot." The good doctor tells us that by running an hour a day, six days a week, one can be immune to coronary disease. Dr. Bassler is at one extreme, just as those who suggest that jogging is "mass suicide" are at another.

Before exploring the tangible benefits to your health from jogging—and there might be enough to save your life—heed the words of Dr. George Sheehan, noted author and a pretty darned good runner:

"When we expose play to the function of promoting

fitness and preventing heart attacks we change its gold to dross. What we need is to conserve those mysterious and elusive elements of play which make it its own reward. If we become fit and impervious to heart attacks and all those other dread diseases, it will be because we don't care if we drop dead doing what we like to do."

Philosophical, yes. Impractical, maybe. But it describes the natural evolution of most of those who get hooked on running. They have long since forgotten why they took it up. Their bodies feel good, and look good. Their self-image has improved, and, mostly, they join increasing numbers who look at running not as exercise, but as therapy. Literally, these people run away from the tension and pressures our society has put upon them. But, even though you may forget your body on a nice, easy jog, you're doing it some good.

Your Heart

Research has proved that fewer heart attacks occur in countries whose populations have a high level of physical activity either through work or play and a low level of saturated fats in their diets. The American Heart Association concludes than an exercise program can probably decrease your chances of sustaining a heart attack or having another if you have already been stricken. Furthermore, if you have a heart attack at all, it will probably be milder if you are physically fit.

What is fitness? The American Heart Association defines it as a state of body efficiency which enables a person to exercise vigorously for a long time-period without fatigue and to respond to sudden physical and emotional demands with an economy of heartbeats and only a modest rise in blood pressure. It concludes that a fit person feels better, sleeps better and supposedly has improved digestion and disposition. So, as you strengthen your heart there is a corresponding lowering of both blood pressure and heart rate so the heart needs less oxygen. Too, research suggests that the way the body handles carbohydrates is improved, and there is less adrenalin-type chemical secreted by the body in response to emotional stress than in the unfit person. The blood's clotting power is also improved so that it is less likely a clot will form on the lipid plaques in the coronary arteries, a condition that should it happen can lead to a heart attack.

So if we believe that it is advantageous to be physically fit—and we should—then how do we become fit? Are race-car drivers—tremendous athletes whose skill and reactions are put on the line to save their lives—physically fit? Probably not, not in the cardiovascular sense unless they also train to enhance their endurance. The trick, of course, is to do enough exercise to improve the cardiovascular system without doing too much to create serious fatigue problems which could result in a serious illness at worst, or in disliking and consequently dropping the activity at best. There is an amount of exercise which is enough to condition the muscles of the body in general and the cardiovascular system in particular that leads to physical fitness, but that is not overly strenuous. There is a target zone in which there is enough activity to achieve fitness, but not too much to exceed safety limits.

According to the American Heart Association, a person's target zone is a heart beating between 70 and 85 percent of his own maximal heart rate. The target zone is enough to give your heart and body a good workout, but not too much to force you to exercise without the body receiving an adequate supply of oxygen. Joggers will quickly become aware of the term aerobic, and the book *Aerobics*, written by Dr. Kenneth Cooper, the man who warned America in the 1960s that it had better exercise, or else. The term aerobic is important. It means that the heart and lungs are supplying enough oxygen to meet the body's demands. Aerobic exercises stimulate the heart and lungs to increase their capacity to meet the body's needs. Once the need surpasses the capacity—the heart and lungs are no longer able to supply adequate oxygen to the muscles—

then you are exercising anaerobically. Or, as athletes say, you have put your body in "oxygen debt." Anyone sprinting a 100-yard dash quickly puts his body in oxygen debt. A great runner like Steve Prefontaine talked about "hitting the wall" about three-fourths of the way through a record-setting 5,000 meters. It's a painful experience an athlete must push himself to for outstanding results; it's something you should avoid.

Before you check your pulse, compute your target zone, and take off, there need be some words of caution. If you are male and between the ages of 40 and 50, realize that there is at least a 50-50 chance that you will already have significant narrowing of one major coronary artery. Exercise is physical stress. And while it is obvious that a normal heart gets stronger with exercise, it is just as obvious that a sick heart can stop under too much stress. Running, when done reasonably and with care, is not dangerous to a person free from disease. Consequently, we recommend that anyone over 35 years of age have a physical examination before embarking on a jogging program. The test should include, if possible, a stress electrocardiogram (ECG), not just the more conventional test taken with your body at rest.

Such a test would indicate your maximal attainable heart rate. But since a stress test is not available to everyone, it is possible to chart your maximal attainable heart rate based on national averages for different ages. Then a subsequent check of your pulse rate will tell you where your target zone—70 to 85 percent of your maximal heart rate—should be.

As an example, a 20-year-old man has a maximal heart rate of 200 based, of course, on national averages. His target zone would then be 140 (70 percent) to 170 (85 percent) heart beats per minute. A 65-year-old man with a maximal attainable heart rate of 150 beats per minute, however, would have a target zone of 107 (70 percent) to 130 (85 percent) beats per minute.

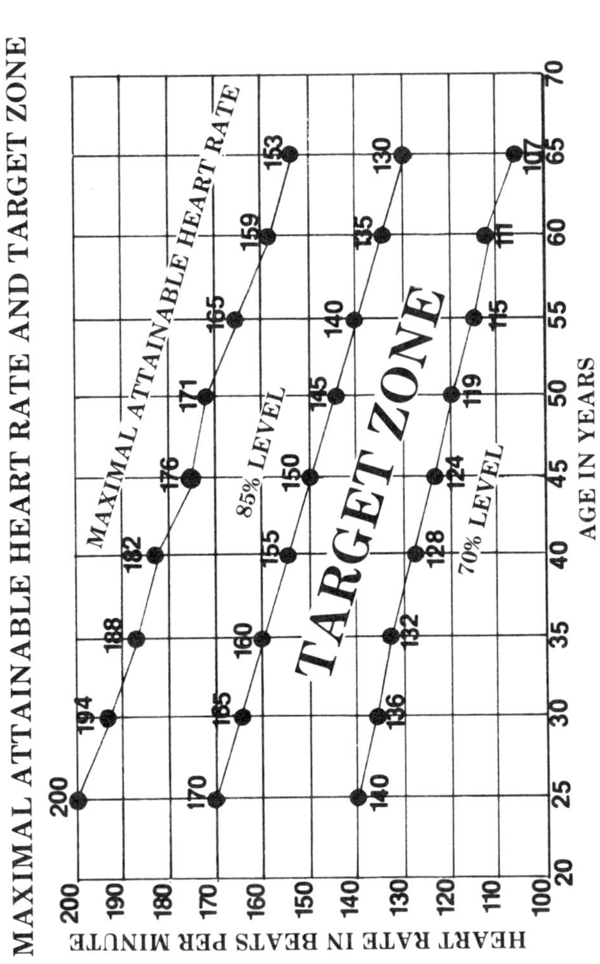
MAXIMAL ATTAINABLE HEART RATE AND TARGET ZONE
MAXIMAL ATTAINABLE HEART RATE
85% LEVEL
TARGET ZONE
70% LEVEL
HEART RATE IN BEATS PER MINUTE
AGE IN YEARS
200
194
188
182
176
171
165
159
153
170
165
160
155
150
145
140
135
130
140
136
132
128
124
119
115
111
107
200
190
180
170
160
150
140
130
120
110
100
20
25
30
35
40
45
50
55
60
65
70

Dr. Lenore R. Zohman, in a booklet entitled "Beyond Diet . . . Exercise Your Way to Fitness and Heart Health," contends that 20 to 30 minutes in the target zone will provide a significant conditioning effect on the cardiovascular system. She cautions that the period of stress in the target zone should be preceded by a warmup of 5 to 10 minutes so the heart and circulatory system are not suddenly and dangerously taxed. This is a period, obviously, when your muscles can be stretched and warmed up. The exercise should be followed by another warming down period at the conclusion of the 20 or 30 minutes in the target zone.

Dr. Zohman contrasts isometric exercises—those like weight lifting which cause muscles to strengthen and shorten—to those which are isotonic, or dynamic. Jogging is dynamic because it requires continuous movement of the legs and results in rhythmic tensing and relaxing of muscles which aids the flow of blood and promotes cardiovascular fitness.

It is her conclusion and that of the American Heart Association that dynamic, aerobic exercise must be carried out three times weekly with no more than two days elapsing between workouts, or gains will begin to be lost.

Obviously, jogging answers the need for physical exercise, both in terms of improvement of your cardiovascular condition, but also as an inexpensive, convenient activity for those who don't have a tennis partner, who don't have access to a swimming pool, or who don't want to take the risks of downhill skiing.

The President's Council on Physical Fitness and Sports asked seven medical experts to evaluate 14 sports and exercises in terms of their contribution to physical well-being. Each activity was scored on a scale of zero to three, thus a rating of 21 for an exercise means that it offers the most benefit. It's important to note that the ratings are based on vigorous exercise of from 30 minutes to an hour at least four times a week. For the golfers, the ratings are based on the use of a cart or a caddy. If you carry your

	Stamina	Muscular Endurance	Muscular Strength	Flexibility	Balance	Weight Control	Muscle Definition	Digestion	Sleep	**Total Score**
JOGGING	21	20	17	9	17	21	14	13	16	**148**
BICYCLING	19	18	16	9	18	20	15	12	15	**142**
SWIMMING	21	20	14	15	12	15	14	13	16	**140**
SKATING (ice or roller)	18	17	15	13	20	17	14	11	15	**140**
HANDBALL/SQUASH	19	18	15	16	17	19	11	13	12	**140**
SKIING—Cross Country	19	19	15	14	16	17	12	12	15	**139**
SKIING—Downhill	16	18	15	14	21	15	14	9	12	**134**
BASKETBALL	19	17	15	13	16	19	13	10	12	**134**
TENNIS	16	16	14	14	16	16	13	12	11	**128**
CALISTHENICS	10	13	16	19	15	12	18	11	12	**126**
WALKING	13	14	11	7	8	13	11	11	14	**102**
GOLF	8	8	9	8	8	6	6	7	6	**66**
SOFTBALL	6	8	7	9	7	7	5	8	7	**64**
BOWLING	5	5	5	7	6	5	5	7	6	**51**

Walking cannot be overestimated as an enjoyable activity involving the basic discipline needed for a successful jogging program.

own bag and walk, the value of golf is much greater.

It seems quite clear, then, that a 20- to 30-mile jog three or four times a week will satisfy your desire to become physically fit.

Remember, however, that physical fitness doesn't happen overnight. Twenty minutes in the target zone is a goal, not an immediate objective. If you are overweight, diet before you begin your jogging program. Or, better yet, begin a program of brisk walking before you think about running. Walking cannot be overestimated as an activity. A brisk 20-minute walk burns only slightly fewer calories than a slow 20-minute run. Your heart rate is likely to exceed 100 beats per minute and approach the target zone. Walking is enjoyable—as running soon should be—and involves the basic discipline needed to begin and maintain a successful jogging program.

You will see that our beginning jogging program is structured around 20 minutes of physical activity each day, even if it is only a 20-minute walk in the beginning. We believe it can take as long as 10 weeks for a person to advance to a level of physical fitness that will allow him to jog continuously for 20 minutes. And we recognize, too, that some may never be able to run continuously for 20 minutes. But if those who can't can safely combine some parts of the activity for 20 minutes each day—even if it is just a brisk 20-minute walk—they will be enhancing their state of physical fitness as well as drawing on the emotional and psychological benefits of daily activity. Easy does it.

Your Body

Yes, it is true that jogging is not the panacea to physical fitness. Your heart and lungs will grow stronger, your leg muscles will develop, you'll probably lose some weight and jettison some tensions. But it won't put you on Muscle Beach, nor will it aid the flexibility and range of motion which becomes so important to those passing through middle age.

As Dr. Stan James, a renowned Eugene orthopedic surgeon and, himself, an addicted jogger, said, "a lot of joggers who put in heavy mileage have very poor muscle tone in their upper body compared to their legs." It was just for that reason that we added the parcours to Pre's Trail, our outstanding jogging facility. The parcours has exercise stations along the trail consisting of a stretch bar platform, a horizontal ladder, a pole climb, a bar jump, a balance beam, and a set of parallel bars.

There is no question, too, that jogging tightens certain leg muscles, and there is an obvious need for stretching exercises to keep the body's full range of motion. Additionally, some joggers complain that they can't maintain a

The parcours on Pre's Trail includes exercise stations designed to strengthen body parts you neglect if you do nothing but jog.

running program because of too much leg and/or back pain. Joggers tend to strengthen their back, hamstring, and calf muscles, sometimes to an imbalance. There is need for a supplemental exercise program, or at least the normal stretching exercises before and after a run that we will discuss later in Chapter 4, "Keeping the Jogger Healthy." The National Jogging Association, which recommends you jog a minimum of 30 minutes a day at least four times a week, advocates an exercise plan it calls The Basic 7. Included are some of the exercises we will discuss later: the hamstring stretcher, the heels-down stretch of the calf muscles and the Achilles tendon, plus such muscle builders as situps, hip hyperextensions, arm rotations, and leg raisers from a sitting position to strengthen the knees.

Few can stretch like youngsters do, but anything aiding flexibility and range of motion helps those passing through middle age.

Another good supplement to a jogging program is the Royal Canadian Air Force exercise plan for physical fitness. A very gradual, long-range program designed to eliminate soreness and fatigue from exercising, the RCAF routine ends each session with a stationary run, which can easily be replaced by your daily jog. There are programs designed for both men and women, but both rely heavily on situps, pushups, chest and leg raises, arm circling, and a stretching exercise such as touching your toes in various stages of difficulty.

The Royal Canadian Air Force developed its plan long before the current surge to become physically fit. But basically it reached the same conclusions we're reaching today: The physically fit person is able to withstand fatigue for longer periods than the unfit; the physically fit person is better equipped to tolerate physical stress; the physically fit person has a stronger and more efficient heart; and there is a relationship between good mental alertness, absence of nervous tension, and physical fitness.

Why Others Say We Shouldn't Run

As jogging becomes a popular activity in America, there are those who are quick to warn us of its ills. And they are to be listened to, within reason.

Reason, of course, must be the guideline all of us follow as we seek physical fitness. We would be the last to preach jogging as the salvation of mankind. Or as the best exercise for people. Or as the only exercise for people. Or that the more you do the more fit you become. In jogging's case, more isn't necessarily better.

"For men and women, running or jogging is one of the most wasteful and hazardous forms of exercise," wrote Dr. J.E. Schmidt in the March, 1976, issue of *Playboy*. Schmidt attempted to make the point that the constant pounding of jogging can weaken the sacroiliac joint, produce herniated or slipped discs, enlarge the veins of the legs leading to phlebitis, and to what he calls a "dropped stomach," "loose spleen," "floating kidney," and "fallen arches." In women, he contended that jogging can lead to sagging breasts, and a "loosely fixed uterus" can be damaged.

The doctors associated with jogging—notably Dr. George Sheehan and Dr. Joan Ullyot—quickly rejected Schmidt's claims as not worth taking seriously. "I think he's being facetious," said Bill Bowerman of Schmidt's article. Medically, there was no published support for the *Playboy* article.

Recently, cases of athletic pseudonephritis, or jogger's kidney, have been detected among some who run strenuously for an hour or more. Basically, under normal conditions, some 20 percent of the blood pumped from the heart flows to the kidneys for filtration and removal of wastes. Exercise causes the body to shunt more blood to the muscles, reducing the flow to the kidneys by as much as 50 percent and in some cases causing an abnormal presence of protein, red blood cells, and other substances in the urine. Jogger's kidney usually cures itself within 48 hours, but whether it can lead to more permanent damage remains to be determined. And until it is, Gilbert Gleim of the Institute of Sports Medicine at New York's Lenox Hill Hospital, say fitness freaks should keep on running or jogging. The known benefits of such exercise, he says, far outweigh any known disadvantages.

And the point is well taken. Most problems that have developed among joggers are found in those who are so physically unfit that jogging is too strenuous, or in those who zealously and imprudently attempt to run too far or too fast.

Obviously, there is a certain amount of pounding and jarring of the body in jogging. If your knees can't handle the pounding, then perhaps you ought to consider swimming. Or bicycling. It's exercise that is important. But before you rule out jogging, realize that some people develop injuries because they have improper equipment, or because they run on their toes, or because they run too far.

We believe in Chapter 4, "Keeping the Jogger Healthy," we answer the questions about equipment and technique. And that, if followed, our running programs will keep you from running too far or too fast.

But your body is different from any other body in this world. Learn to listen to what it is telling you. After a while, it will tell you if your running shoes are inadequate, if your shorts are too tight, if your foot-strike is improper, or if you're running too far.

Approach exercise with your body in mind. All the research on possible injuries from jogging is far from in. But do you have time to wait until it is in? You can obviously strengthen your heart and minimize coronary disease. You can also keep tabs on your weight, improve your self-image, and enjoy the emotional benefits of exercise. We think it's worth a try. And, done with reason, it is worth any potential risks that might be lurking under a microscope or in the future. Man, before the automobile, ran and walked. It is not an activity foreign to our bodies. Or at least it shouldn't be.

3

The Philosophy of Jogging

Of all the statistics and claims which swirl around the jogging craze, one may be more important than all the rest. According to the National Jogging Association, 90 percent of those who begin jogging this year won't be jogging next year. And despite all the benefits which may be derived from jogging, there is no carryover effect. The miles you ran yesterday will do you no good next year. So any discussion of a jogging philosophy must concern itself with what makes some joggers fit, and others quit and not fit.

"Never make it ugly," says one Eugene jogger. "Learn to read your body and do what it says," says another. "I've experienced discomfort," says a third, "but I've never known real pain. I'll stop before it hurts."

The mind, not the legs, not the lungs, not the heart, will determine if you are a jogger, and what type of jogger you will be. First, the mind must make the commitment to put you on display. Ten, 15 years ago, you might have held yourself up to public ridicule or arrest as Bill Bowerman was on a nightly run from the track coaches' meeting in

Learn to run alone, for the first commitment to jog is a personal one.

New Mexico to his nearby hotel. People laughed and questioned his sanity. Today, I think, they quietly admire the jogger, and question their own conviction and direction. With changing ideals and a society that has suddenly put physical fitness and good health as a top priority, it is likely that friends and neighbors will envy rather than ridicule you. And as you run free and easy past those who choose the sedentary life, you will have a surge of pride in the commitment—not lip service, but real commitment—you have made to improving your health and appearance.

Although much has been made of the social benefits of jogging—the camaraderie and goodwill which comes with group runs—the first commitment is a personal one. You cannot depend on peer pressure to make you jog. Business appointments will quickly keep you from the group run.

Or if not business appointments, then rain, snow, heat, humidity, sleet, wind, or a personality conflict with someone you would rather not share a drop of sweat with.

Jog because you want to jog. Learn to run alone. Later, you can break up the routine or celebrate your progress with a group run. And it may work out that you regularly run with others. But, in the beginning, it is your mind, your body, and your program.

The metamorphosis of a static, slightly overweight non-athlete to a once-a-day jogger is dramatic. But also lengthy. Every source indicates that it takes at least a month, and more probably three months, to reach a state of physical fitness that will allow you to run free and easy. Frank Shorter, the Olympic marathon champion, says, "try running for a month. If by then you don't think it's fun, take up another sport." At some point, however, the dawning of a new day will occur. An advertisement for running shoes captured the feeling you will chase:

"Sooner or later the serious runner goes through a special, very personal experience that is unknown to most people. Some call it euphoria. Others say it's a new kind of mystical experience that propels you into an elevated state of consciousness. A flash of joy. A sense of floating as you run. And from that point on, there is no finish line. You run for your life."

All of which sounds pretty good. Remember, however, the people who wrote that are selling shoes. Others will too often recite it to you with the fervor of an evangelist. In the beginning, at least, avoid the running zealots. Develop a joy of running on your own terms. You'll know the feeling the first time two miles is a breeze. That you aren't aware of the distance you've covered, or how hard you were breathing, or how your legs felt. It happens to different people in different ways, and at different times. But there is no question that you must endure in the beginning.

So it is that the most important steps you will take are those first ones. The results of those first few jogs may well

The best way to check your condition and pace while running is the talk test. If you can't talk, then you're running too fast.

determine whether you quit and join the 90 percent, or stay and run with the 10 percent who love running, because if they didn't, they wouldn't keep doing it. We have developed a beginners' jogging program that, starting from scratch, will tell you how far, how fast, how often. Much, obviously, will depend on your present physical condition. The best start is always a slow start. A brisk walking program will burn calories, get the heart beat up, and provide the discipline and self-assurance you need to begin jogging. Or, as many do, start by combining short jogs with intervals of brisk walks.

There are a number of ways to monitor your progress, a check of your heart beat being one. Check it in the morning when you first awake. It's a convenient time to do it, and also the time when your body is most at rest. In time, you should notice a steady decrease in the resting heart rate. You can also test it right after a run, and then minutes later to detect your recovery rate. The easiest and best method for checking your condition during a run, however, is Coach Bowerman's time-tested talk test. You may conclude after the first few runs that it is ridiculous to even consider talking during a run because you are quickly impressed with the need to conserve every ounce of breath and energy just to make your appointed rounds. If that is the case, then you have missed the point. You are obviously running a mile to run a mile, not running to enjoy the therapeutic benefits of running, not running to slowly and painlessly work into a state of being physically fit, not running within yourself to avoid possible over-exertion, and not running to insure yourself that you'll still be running next year.

Medically, the talk test will insure you that your activity is aerobic, meaning that the heart and lungs are supplying sufficient oxygen to meet the body's demands. If you are out of breath while you run, then it may well be that you are operating anaerobically and that your body is in oxygen debt. Such a situation does your body no good, and will only leave you completely exhausted. Besides, if the goal is to put your heart beat into the target zone for 20 minutes or more a day—and leave it there—then what's your hurry? Slow, easy running over two or three miles is both more pleasant and more beneficial than a tough, competitive mile for a guy or gal who a month earlier couldn't even run one. Medically and psychologically it is better to run, we think, three miles in 30 minutes than one mile in six minutes. And, let's face it, not all of us have the body type that would allow us to run a six-minute mile. Speed and athletic ability need not be factors.

Coach Bowerman made the point from the very begin-

The morning joggers stumble out of bed, dress stiff bodies, fight rain, cold, and darkness, but would have it no other way.

ning, and made it above all others: Train, don't strain. Please don't overdo it, he'll say to this day. And the best test for that is still the talk test. If a slow jog is too fast for conversation, then you should be walking. If you're running alone, try talking to yourself. Or even whistling, that can be a good test of your aerobic capacity.

When and where you run is up to you. But find a time that fits your lifestyle and agrees with your body, and then stay with it. The morning joggers stumble out of bed, dress stiff and disgusted bodies, fight cold, rain, and darkness, but wouldn't do it any other way. It is their special time of the day. When the work day starts, their engines are warmed and running smoothly. There is no trouble waking up. Three miles through your awakening neighborhood allows time to organize your day, sort out problems, or just put your mind in neutral. Perhaps you become preoccupied with the morning world of the neighborhood dogs, or the garbagemen, or maybe you have a pleasant rural run where you can watch the water level of a winter creek, admire the first disclosures of sunrise, or horses grazing in a field. Others simply can't handle the morning stiffness, or just the thought of getting up any earlier than they already must. Perhaps those joggers have the opportunity to pass on the martini lunch and can spend the noon hour running. Or they run, as many do, in the period after work and before dinner. Variety should spice the places where you run, but your time of the day should become routine. Places vary as drastically as do personalities. Some like the routine and regularity of the local high school track. Others disdain the track so completely that they'll run streets, sidewalks, anywhere to avoid the monotony of going round and round. Some mix the two quite well. In the beginning, pick something reasonably level. Hills often highlight the course of an experienced jogger, but the beginner can aggravate leg problems running up and down hills. If you want the distance of your course measured, drive your car along the route, checking the mileage with the odometer. Some runners would rather not know their distance, and check their progress only by time. Later, as they settle into a comfortable pace they can compute the mileage by elapsed time. Neither the awareness of time nor mileage is essential, however. Some days you might want to run two miles but end up only running one. On another you might be out for a 10-minute run, discover that as you near the tenth minute your body is beginning to bounce, that your thoughts are far from either time or distance, or soreness or pain, and you want to run twice as far. Do it.

For the sake of physical fitness, you should run a minimum of every other day, or three times a week. The National Jogging Association suggests four times a week. In the beginning, however, it is often easier to run each day of the week, allowing, however, for one day a week of

Allot plenty of time to exercise, take your time warming up, run relaxed and without the pressure of time or competition.

rest. It takes time before running is both fun and routine. Running every day eliminates the decision-making process. The one day of rest can be planned, or it can be the day it becomes impossible for you to squeeze in your exercise period.

One of the most well-known facets of our training program for distance runners at Oregon is the hard-easy approach. We have never stressed a lot of miles for our distance runners, and we always vary their workouts so that a hard day is followed by an easy one. For Dyrol Burleson, who was very strong, his week consisted of two hard days followed by one very easy one. Kenny Moore, on the other hand, thrived on one hard day followed by two easy ones. Our program for the beginning jogger is approached in the same way. If two miles represents a long run for you, then rest the next day or go for an easy one-mile jog. It's worked for world-class distance runners, and it can work for you.

Joe Henderson, editor of the popular *Runner's World* magazine, is the leading advocate of the run-gently, run-long method of jogging. Convincingly, he contests the theories of Dr. Meyer Friedman, who in his best-seller *Type A Behavior and the Heart* calls jogging "mass suicide." Henderson and Friedman agree on one point: If running is tied to a sense of urgency, it can be dangerous to the Type A personality, the aggressive, goal-oriented person who becomes a prime candidate for a heart attack because of the inordinate pressure put on him by himself. For a person who labors under the burden of constant time demands to add yet another demand on his time is only inviting trouble.

"The kind of running-jogging recommended in most texts for beginners—the 10-15 minutes every other day is a common prescription—is enough to give a quick, violent workout but probably not enough to form a lasting habit," writes Henderson in the *Long Run Solution*, the solution consisting of long, slow runs where time and competition are irrelevant. But, Henderson, too, understands the problems a person has in reaching the mental and physical endurance needed to run for 20 or 30 minutes.

"Those first 10 to 20 minutes of a run are rather distasteful preliminaries—for everyone, seasoned runners as well as beginners," he writes. "It takes this long to convince yourself that you're serious about working, and that the body should cooperate. . . . This is why I say the sooner you make a habit of going well beyond 20 minutes a day, the better you'll feel. I recommend a half-hour of movement, every day from day one on, even if you have to walk all or most or some of it. Loosely fit the half-hour of movement into a full hour you've blocked out for yourself. . . . Give half of it to activity, half to inactivity, and don't hurry through either one."

For those of us who find a need to flee stresses and tensions of everyday life—which is our 20th century life—jogging can provide an adequate release. Our ancestors labored on farms, or on ships, or in mills, or in mines. They were too tired to be tense. They slept well because they were physically spent from a physically demanding day's work. Frankly, they didn't need to jog.

But if we realize that our bodies and our minds miss the demands of physical work, then we must also realize that we of the 20th century are trying to escape urgency and competition. Hard work was the result of 19th century labor; urgency and stress are the result of ours. It doesn't mean we should avoid all competition—the weekend road run can be a great measuring rod for our progress as well as satisfying the competitive urge in all of us—but the daily jog should be a time to relax your mind, ignite your body and let the two forces produce a pleasant, worthwhile experience.

At Oregon, we give our runners a written philosophy of running. Although geared to the competitive athlete, the principles are applicable to you, the jogger. One of our main concerns at Oregon is that a distance runner will reach his potential too early. We don't want him peaking during his college career. We have long felt that the competitive life of a distance runner may well cover a period of two decades. We want the runners to keep running, just as we want you to keep jogging. Longevity should be an important goal of both the runner and the jogger. These, then, are our principles.

Principle 1: Moderation—We believe that moderation should apply to all facets of a runner's life. I learned this the hard way. In September, 1963, I decided to make a comeback after a three-year layoff. My goal was to make our Olympic team in the 5,000 meters for the Tokyo Olympics in 1964. The popular concept at that time was that running 120 miles a week was the key to success. I started out on a 120-mile-a-week program and lasted about eight weeks. Even though I was tired, I found myself running 17 miles a day, simply to get in my mileage. I eventually reached a point where I was unable to train because of illness brought on by continued fatigue. If 120 miles a week was the secret to running, we could all be Olympic champions. I tell runners: "Let common sense rule; use moderation."

Principle 2: Progression—An individual's progression can be controlled by what we call "date pace" and "goal pace." In most cases, the toughest part of training is holding back so that you will not peak too soon. Keep your running under wraps. Both the runner and the jogger must be aware of both his goal and his limitations. In establishing a goal pace for our runners, we ask them to consider their experience as a competitive runner. We ask each of them what his goal is for the year. In many cases it is a compromise between what he thinks he is capable of doing and our evaluation of his ability. I vividly remember my talk with Steve Prefontaine when he entered Oregon as a freshman. When asked for his goal in the mile for his freshman year, he replied. "3:48.0" At that time he was a 4:06 high school miler. Needless to say, we liked the confidence he had, but managed to convince him that he was expecting too much for a one-year jump. Through compromise we ended up with a goal of 3:56 for his freshman year. He ended up the season running 3:57.1. The date pace, goal pace method of training can be of value to the jogger who wants to improve his performance, and in the training for a marathon. In Chapter 8, "Beyond Jogging," the date pace, goal pace method used in Oregon runners will be made available to you. In essence, this method involves interval training. There are other ways to check progression, but in most cases runners find need of a diary or a runner's log. I kept one throughout my training for the Olympics, and still refer to it for writing workouts for our runners. The jogger will find it fun and also worthwhile. He will quickly understand why he's not feeling well, or the effect of hills, or track workouts, or cold days on his running. He should note the distance, the time of day, the weather, the terrain, and pay particular attention to any soreness or injury that might be cropping up. It helps you remember what your body was saying after each run.

Principle 3: Adaptability—Good common sense is needed in adapting a running program for each individual. Weather, terrain, facilities, health of the individual and many other unforseen circumstances will truly test one's ingenuity as a runner. In 1957, I was in the Air Force and stationed at a remote radar site on the northern tip of the Olympic Peninsula in Washington. It was 80 miles to the nearest town that had a track. So I had to adapt. I developed a method of doing intervals on the beach by counting my strides. I would count to myself each time my right foot touched down until I reached 10. I would then put one finger out to keep track. I would continue this process for the equivalent of 12 fingers, estimating this to be approximately 440 yards. I would run up and down this stretch of beach doing 220s, 330s, 440s, 880s, 1320s by what I call the count system. I used this system for eight months of training without ever stepping on a track, never knowing exactly how far I was running or how fast. The first time I stepped on a track the following spring for a test effort I ran a 4:05 mile. I went on that year to set American records in the 1,500 meters, 2-mile, 3-mile, and 5,000 meters. To this day, as a jogger, I find myself occasionally counting to myself as my right foot touches the ground. In developing a beginners' jogging program, we have used this count system that was developed on a lonely beach in the state of Washington. But, more importantly, it showed the reason to be adaptable. Anyone who outlines a weekly program of running and carries it through rigidly without this consideration is in trouble.

In developing a jogging philosophy, be your own person. Understand your goals, your body, and your program.

Principle 4: Variation—It's healthy to vary the pattern of running, not anticipating what is coming up the next week. Variation leads to mental freshness. Vary the terrain and the venue. The surface, the weather, the elevation, the company. It all helps.

Principle 5: Callusing—If using a pick and shovel is a new experience for you, there will be a period of adjusting to soreness and blisters before you develop the calluses that make it possible to handle the work efficiently without undue stress. This callusing effect also applies to running. It is not always possible to anticipate all the stresses or unforseen circumstances that can arise in running situations. But before you run a marathon, you should have at least been on a 15- to 18-mile run. In 1956, I decided with the urging of my coach, Bill Bowerman, to run the 5,000 meters rather than the 1,500 meters in our Olympic tryouts. I had won the NCAA championship in the mile in 1954, was the runnerup to a teammate, Jim Bailey, in 1955. The mile was my favorite race, but I had to agree with Bowerman that I had a better chance of making our team in the 5,000 meters. But what a callusing effect. The first 5,000 I ran in competition was the longest, hardest race I had ever run, simply because I was not callused for the distance at that pace.

As you develop a jogging philosophy, learn to run alone, learn to run slowly, learn to listen to your body and react to its warning signals. Be your own person. Understand your goals, your body, and your program. The principles of moderation, progression, adaptability, variation, and callusing can be important to you in your jogging experience.

4

Keeping the Jogger Healthy

The children of Eugene idolized Steve Prefontaine. Hung on his every word, recited his greatest triumphs. They knew he held every American distance record. And, yet, one of his most important records has been overlooked: In his four years of training and competing as an undergraduate at the University of Oregon, he never missed one day of training or competition because of illness or injury. Certainly, Pre was a rare specimen. But beyond this, I believe his durability and consistent good health stemmed from the steps taken at Oregon to prevent injuries and illness.

Running Shoes

First things first. Although the rewards of jogging can be rich, the financial investment in an activity that can lengthen and enrich your life is small. Realize that when you make your one major purchase: running shoes. You run on your feet and you'll go no farther than they will take you. Respect them.

Figure to spend between $18 and $40 for a pair of shoes.

Stick with the established companies, ask for a training shoe, get it fitted properly, and you will have few problems.

You wouldn't play golf with a hickory stick; don't run in Hush Puppies. There are three prerequisites for a good jogging shoe: A soft sole which gives ample protection for the ball of the foot, a supportive arch, and a heel that is wide enough to offer a good base and is raised at least a half-inch.

The shoes you wear every day have a raised heel. To suddenly run in one without a raised heel will produce soreness in the Achilles tendon and calf muscles. The wide base at the heel keeps the foot from rocking from side to side as you run. Ask for a training shoe, not a running flat. Shoe stores, of course, are proliferating at a rate equal to the jogging boom. Shop around. Find a store where your individual needs are met, where the shoe is properly fitted and concern is taken that your arch is properly supported and there is room for your toes to move. Popular models in Eugene include the Nike waffle trainer—one developed by Bill Bowerman from a design inspired by Mrs. Bowerman's waffle iron—and the New Balance 320, which many of our Oregon runners have switched to because the New Balance shoe is offered in different widths. Nationally, the Brooks Vantage, the Adidas Runner, the Etonic Street Fighter, the Puma Easy Rider and the Tiger Grand Prix are either popular or highly regarded, or both.

The traditional canvas gym shoe is heavy, and offers little support for the heel and the ball of the foot. There are many cheap imitations of the training shoe—seeming to meet all the needs—but the question of durability is there. Will they withstand the pounding? And, more importantly, will your feet?

Technique

Hopefully, you are not reviewing this chapter to see what went wrong. Prevention, not treatment, is paramount to the recreation runner who doesn't have the advantage of a coach and trainer, and who doesn't want to interrupt training with costly jogs to the doctor.

A majority of the injuries to foot, ankle, leg, knee, and hip are a direct result of improper running technique. Overstriding and running on the ball of the foot create most of the problems. You are not sprinting. Don't relive the day you ran anchor at the Penn Relays. The runner whose foot strike is on the ball of the foot rather than the heel could bring on a case of shin splints, or even a stress fracture of the foot. The heel hits first, then the ball of the foot. If it is impossible for you to get off your toes, then seek out soft surfaces for training as well as a shoe with extra padding, or add padding to the shoe you have.

Shin splints prey on the sprinter, but may hit every runner from time to time. Generally, our medical people indicate they are caused by a poor shoe, or too much time spent running on hard surfaces. Shin splints indicate a soreness somewhere between the ankle and the knee on the front or sides of the leg. If your legs are a little tender after a long run, massage the area with ice to reduce the inflammation.

We have an exercise to prevent shin splints by stretching the muscles in the front of the leg. From a sitting position—a chair or the edge of the bed will do fine—cross one leg over the other. Then use your hands to work the foot around in all positions, force it beyond its normal range of motion to achieve maximum stretching of these muscles. One minute daily on each foot could prevent a case of shine splints.

Another improper bit of running technique common to the jogger and competitive runner alike is overstriding. Running with too long a stride is inefficient. And besides sapping energy, it can eventually lead to knee and hip problems. How many times have you heard someone urge, "Lengthen your stride" to pick up the pace? Let's examine what happens when you lengthen your stride. Quickly, the center of gravity of the body is put between the two legs, forcing the trailing leg to produce extra effort to pull the unbalanced weight back up and over for the next stride. Each time the foot strikes the ground the center of gravity of your body should be directly above the strike of the foot. The longer the run, the more important this becomes. Overstriding can be corrected by constantly reminding yourself to concentrate on a shorter stride. If you want to pick up the pace, shorten your stride and quicken your leg speed. Don't reach out.

Posture and hip position also are important in preventing injuries and developing an efficient stride. Run with an attitude of running tall. Lift the rib cage and run as vertical as possible to help achieve this feeling.

Also, the pelvis should be tilted up for efficiency of leg movement. Develop this by standing against a wall, tightening your abdominal muscles and touching the small of your back against the wall. The pelvis must tilt up to

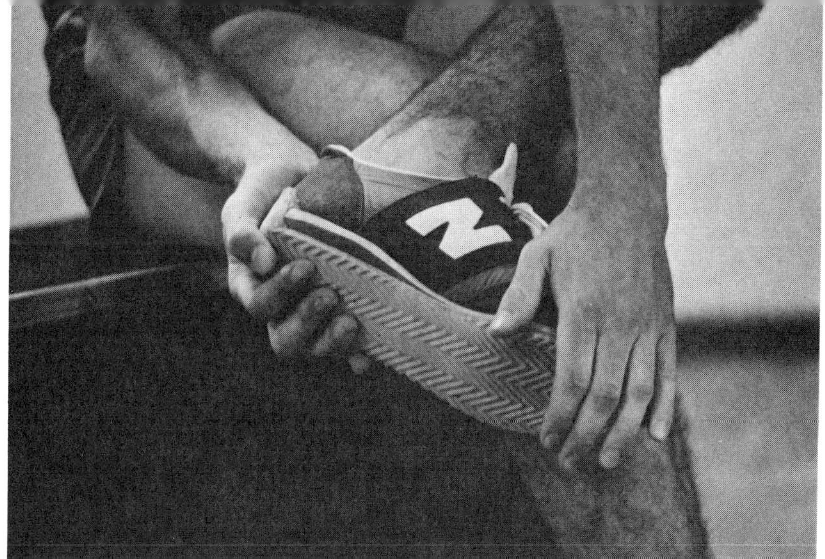

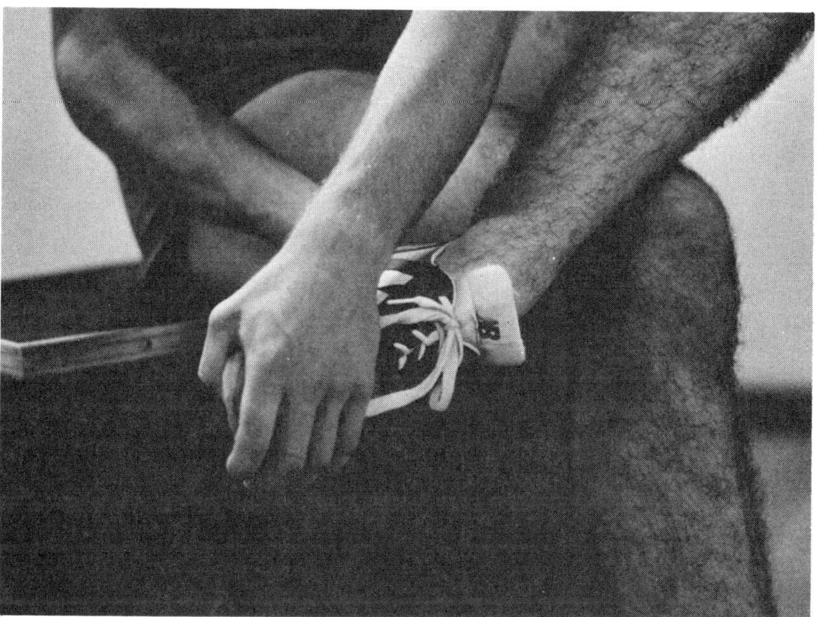

To prevent shin splints, use your hand to work the foot around in all positions, forcing it beyond its normal range of motion.

To lift the pelvis and strengthen the stomach muscles, lie on your back, force the small of it to the floor by tightening the abdominals; slowly lift the legs.

accomplish this. Ever notice the well-developed and clearly defined abdominal muscles of a distance runner? This is a valuable by-product of holding the pelvis in the correct position while running. To let the abdominal muscles sag will put pressure on the lower-back region and may eventually lead to lower-back problems.

A good exercise to lift the pelvis and strengthen the stomach muscles is to lie on your back and force the small of the back to the floor by tightening the abdominals. Slowly lift the legs together off the floor and hold to a 30 count. Begin by bending the knees when lifting the legs.

But your goal can be to eventually go through this drill with legs locked straight.

Unfortunately, there is no honeymoon period for the runner. Almost immediately you will develop muscle soreness. Because you don't have a trainer or a coach, be analytical. When your body is sore it is telling you something is wrong. Find out what it is.

It makes sense for the beginning jogger to have good shoes, and to start oh-so-slowly. A running club in San Francisco puts its motto on the wall: Start Slow and Then Taper Off. Don't begin your early runs on uneven or hilly terrain. The runner who immediately runs hills will quickly develop problems because his Achilles tendons are not stretched out, and neither are his calf muscles. His hamstrings will be sore and so will his toes from sliding in his shoes. Start on a flat course, and, if possible, on something softer than concrete. A neophyte runner pounding streets and sidewalks is a candidate for shin splints. A golf course, a trail through the woods, a grassy athletic field at the local high school, or even a facility like our Pre's Trail is preferable to the streets or a hard track. In any case, you should alternate the types of surfaces on which you run, both for your mind, and your feet and legs.

Stretching

All beginning runners will have general soreness that lasts four or five days and then begins to go away. It's caused basically by a buildup of lactic acid. Jogging can be a wonderful activity, but understand that your body will show some signs of early resistance. Muscles in the legs become stronger, all right, but they also become tighter and shorter. They need to be stretched before you can use them comfortably and safely. Our medical people have determined with increasing evidence that if your muscles have a good range of motion and are properly stretched there is a significant decrease in injury. The best routine might be a half-mile or so warmup with a slow jog, a set of stretching exercises, and then off on your run.

Achilles tendonitis is the Number 1 runner's injury. Stretch your Achilles tendons before you run.

Achilles tendonitis ranks No. 1 on the list of runners' injuries. As one grows older he naturally loses the elasticity of the tendons, compounding this problem. At Oregon, our runners use an incline board to help prevent strains of the Achilles and the calf muscles. It's possible to stretch these muscles by stepping forward with one leg and stretching the Achilles in the rear leg by keeping the foot straight in line with the body and the heel firmly on the ground. Lean forward with both hands on the thigh of the forward leg. You can also get in a standing pushup position with a wall or the side of your car, and by slowly leaning forward you can stretch the Achilles if the heels are kept on the ground. We have really come to like the incline board. So much so, in fact, that our runners take them wherever they go. If you should have the opportunity

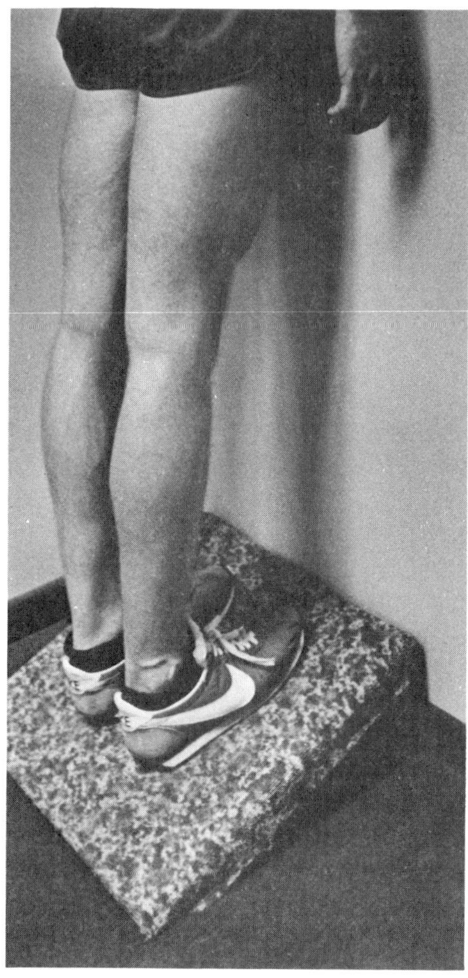

Oregon's runners use an incline board, standing on it for ten minutes before running to stretch the Achilles tendons.

of using something like our incline board, spend 10 minutes in a static stretch of the Achilles tendon. Heels are in contact with the board, knees are bent, and hips are moved toward the wall and kept at a maximum stretch for the full 10 minutes. A second 10 minutes can be used to develop the calf muscles. Simply by straightening the legs into full tension you will transfer the stretch back into the muscles of the calf.

The body makes its own heat when it's working; the trick is to retain some heat. Dress snugly in layers with nothing binding.

Clothing

Although we in Eugene think of our weather as mild and perfectly suited for running, much of the country views us as a damp, cool climate better suited to sitting inside by the fire. Running in the rain can be a joy. Our persistent mist presents few problems. To the contrary, its cooling action is a breath of freshness on a long run.

The body supplies its own heat when it's working. The trick is in retaining some of that heat. Dress in layers.

Wool is best, retaining heat even when wet. Our trainer recommends a light rain suit over your jogging sweats for winter running. Not a rubberized suit which doesn't breathe, but rather a nylon suit with vents to aid circulation.

Your clothing should be snug, but not binding. It is important to keep the muscles warm when you are running. When the temperature dips below 45 degrees, think about wearing clothing to keep your leg muscles warm. As it gets cooler, of course, you must be concerned about your hands, head, and ears. Be comfortable. If your hands are cold, wear gloves. Much heat can be retained by wearing a stocking cap. Despite the old wives' tale about your lungs freezing when it gets really cold, that won't happen. If you want to breathe warmer air, put a scarf over your mouth.

Wind can make it much colder than it seems on a long—or short—winter run. Be aware of the wind-chill factor, which is derived by subtracting the speed of the wind in miles per hour from the temperature. Fifteen degrees Fahrenheit with a 15 mile-per-hour wind creates a chill factor of zero. If the temperature or the chill factor drops to 25 degrees below zero, it is time to seek out that nice warm fire. Frostbite becomes a real possibility.

Heat

The body is much more equipped to cope with cold than it is with heat. When the weather gets warm, wear as little as the law allows. We prefer nylon running shorts and our runners don't wear a jock strap, that traditional piece of equipment which might be fine for basketball players but wasn't designed with the runner in mind. Our runners like jockey shorts as an undergarment, although some wear the new nylon bikini-type briefs. The jock strap can produce chafing, which also occurs in heavy-legged runners. If you develop chafing between your legs, try wearing cotton long johns cut off just above the knees. In any case, put a skin lubricant like Vaseline on all areas that are chafing. Much has been made of the so-called

When the temperature is above 90 degrees, wear as little as the law allows. Soak up all the fluid you can.

jogger's nipples, a chafing condition of the nipples in both men and women. Running bare chested will obviously eliminate the problem, but in lieu of going to jail or freezing to death, either put a skin lubricant on the nipples or cover them with Band-Aids.

Fluids

Force fluids. Drink as much as you can before you run, while you're running, and after you run when the temperature is above 90 degrees. Of all the running conditions you will face, hot weather is the most hazardous. Water is essential in keeping your body temperature down. Don't risk dehydration. We have found that cold water—ice water if it is available—works quickest. The National Jogging Association recommends a drink of diluted orange juice—mixed half-and-half with water—and a sprinkling of salt. Vitamin C and salt are lost when you sweat. Avoid sugared drinks. If the temperature is very high, and you are running for more than 20 minutes, plan to drink along the run. And what you don't drink, toss on your body.

If you become dizzy or nauseated, realize that you are flirting with heatstroke. Stop, find some shade, and replace fluids. Cramping is caused by two things: Fatigue and a change in the body chemistry. We've found that your body is generally lacking in the electrolytes. Salt your food a little more than usual (we aren't all that excited about salt tablets) and be sure to include oranges, bananas, and tomatoes in your diet—they are all high in potassium.

Diet

Jogging contributes to our physical fitness, can produce marvelous mental benefits, and combined with a sensible diet can help you lose weight. But don't for a minute think that running 20 minutes a day will suddenly allow you to eat and drink all you want. Face the fact that running a mile burns up slightly more than 100 calories. Or the number of calories in one of the new light beers. Dr. Ernst van Aaken said it best: "Run slowly, run daily, drink moderately, and don't eat like a pig." Your dietary needs are those of every human—and they should be supplied from natural sources, and not vitamin supplements. Our runners eat five hours before competition and we think you should wait one hour before your jog. Carbohydrates, or course, are easily digested and, personally, I like a bowl of peaches, toast and tea or coffee before a long run.

Don't diet excessively or take diet pills when you are on a running program. Harsh foods—fried foods and those that for other reasons might bother your stomach—should be avoided. Use common sense. You are burning more calories a day if you run than if you don't. Coupled with a common sense diet—something as simple as not eating dessert each night or having one beer after work instead of two—running can cause significant weight loss, a weight loss you can live with and maintain.

If your early goal is to improve your defense against heart disease, then a diet which copes with cholesterol as well as promotes weight reduction is a perfect complement to a jogging program. Again, in moderation.

The American Heart Association recommends that you eat more lean cuts of beef and other meats, plus veal, chicken and turkey. Eat more fish, polyunsaturated margarine and vegetable oils such as corn oil, soybean oil and cottonseed oil, more fat-free milk, skim-milk dairy products and low-fat cheese. On the other hand, you should eat less fatty cuts of beef, lamb and pork, organ meats and eggs (less than three yolks per week.) Less saturated fats, cream, ice cream, butter, lard, whole milk, cheeses and non-diary creamers. The heart association believes that a combination of such a diet and a good exercise program can reduce the possibility of coronary disease. Try it, you might like it.

Remember that injury or sickness will affect your jogging. Don't attempt to train through an injury. Most likely it would result in additional injuries. When you walk without favoring an injury, then you can try to run. Don't rush to make up what you lost, but progress from where you are.

The common cold takes 10 days to run its course. If you insist on hard running through this period, you can bring on secondary infections that may set you back additional days or weeks. If you have a simple cold, either skip your run or cut your distance in half. If you have a temperature, don't run. Do not tear your body down. If you're tired, if you don't really want to run, if you've got the physical blahs, then rest. Occasionally, a three or four day rest will do you wonders. It will literally keep you on the right track.

5

Women on the Move

Connie Manley, wife of an Olympic distance runner, mother of three preschool children, housewife, and runner's widow, had tried to run with her husband but found the experience both disappointing and painful. And yet she sensed a certain well-being among those who were physically fit. She wanted to be slim, to have more energy, to be associated with the athletes she had seen on an extended stay in Europe for the 1972 Olympic Games in Munich. Fitness was one reason Connie Manley began running. Sanity was another.

"My friends used to tease me that I jogged to get away from the kids," she said, "which is probably true. The kids would get to me. So about three days a week I would get a babysitter, and then run from about four to five in the afternoon . . . which was the worst time of the day around the house; it always is for little kids. Things were wild and everybody was on edge.

"And I loved running" she continued. "It was neat to be able to get out and away from that and I would come back and just me being calm would have a good effect on the

"I'm convinced you'll find time to run if you think it is important," says Connie Manley, "and running is a pretty high priority for me."

Connie Manley admits that she runs partly to get away from her children. "When I come back just me being calm has a good effect on the kids."

kids. They were great kids but being with them all day I needed a break."

Connie started out running what she could of a mile loop in her North Eugene neighborhood. "It was hard at first, there's no question about it," she said. "My main aim was trying not to feel too bad. Once I learned to listen to my body, I slowed down. That's what good runners have learned: To listen to their bodies. The rest of us learn it the hard way."

That was 1972. Five years later Connie Manley was still running, she had a part-time teaching job and found herself running between one o'clock in the afternoon and when the kids got home from school at three. The mile loop became a seven-mile run on Pre's Trail, spiced with occasional weekend competitions and in the fall of 1977, at age 35, her first marathon, a very fine three hours and 20 minutes.

"I'm convinced that you'll find time to run if you think it is important," she says. "Running is a pretty high priority for me; it is something I really value doing. After all these years I still think I feel better, I have more energy, and because I like to eat, I feel that I can eat pretty much what I want."

There is, of course, a tremendous growth in the numbers of women jogging. Like many other facets of our society, women are Mary-come-latelies to running. A culture which has for so long been the advocate of personal freedoms somehow forgot the ladies. It has long been believed that women are too dainty, too fragile, too necessary to the everyday operation of the home to waste time exercising. Especially doing something that often produces sweat.

Our jogging paths are crowded with women runners, especially during weekdays. For a man, you had better get used to a lady gliding past you toward the end of a three-mile jaunt or give up running in public. Many women are beautiful, effortless runners who only get stronger and better as the mileage increases. Others are horrible plodders who, nevertheless, are burning calories, developing confidence, and gaining, probably for the first time, an awareness of their bodies under physical stress.

After running her marathon, Connie Manley attended an awards dinner. "There were a couple of guys giving testimonials on running," she said, "and telling how a few years earlier all they could do was run to the cigarette machine. And we were sitting there thinking, 'Oh, my God, it's just like a revival meeting.' That's just too much. People ask me about my running and I try to be matter-of-fact. It's great for people, but not everyone wants to be a runner. There are a lot of other ways to stay fit. But

Many women are beautiful, effortless runners who only get stronger and better as the mileage increases.

running is so easy; I don't need anyone to do it with, I don't need equipment, I don't have to go to the pool or the tennis court. It's just something that is neat for me."

Probably the less said about the differences in men and women runners the better. As more women run, information is proving that there is little difference. If anything, women have more endurance and are better equipped for long, long distances than are men. Remember the long distance swimmers of yesteryear who were women?

Ernst van Aaken, the noted German physiologist, writes, "From statistics going back 100 years, we know that women are more enduring than men. For example, the average life expectancy of women is 73 years, that of men 68. Athletically, the most important difference between men and women is that 40 percent of a man's body mass is muscle, compared with only 23 percent for women. This limits women's strength and speed. On the other hand, women have more subcutaneous fat, and thus have better energy reserves and protection from the cold."

Everywhere, there are examples of women's endurance. Miki Gorman, after her victory in the 1974 Boston Marathon in 2:47, said, "I can't run much faster, but I can run much, much farther. Once I ran 100 miles on the track." Nina Kuscsik, winner of the 1972 women's division of the Boston Marathon, told Jim Fixx in *The Complete Book of Running*, that "in 35 marathons, I've never hit the wall. I get tired, but I can always keep going."

Technique

Thaddeus Kostrubala writes in *The Joy of Running*: "Women seem to run with greater ease than men. Their style is easy. The natural style of most 12-to-14-year-old girls is almost perfect. They roll their feet, their pelvises move. They look at ease and ready to play; in fact, they are playing. Is all this because they have not been the victim of male cultural expectation—that of competition?"

Because many women have never run before, they tend to confuse sprinting and running. Women need to review our instruction on running style, paying particular attention to the strike of the foot—the heel hitting first—and the necessity to keep your weight over the foot which is striking the ground. Remember that it is inefficient to swing your foot into position, and that the knee is a hinge, not a swivel. Some women lean forward too much and carry their arms too high. Remember to run tall.

Clothing

To repeat, the most important piece of clothing and equipment for any runner is a pair of good training flats. The shoe companies realize the proliferation of women runners and are now producing varying styles of shoes for women. Stick with the established companies, ask for a training shoe, get it fitted properly, and you will have few problems. Make the shoe people fit you. Tell them the type of terrain you run on, the distance you go, the price range

Elegance matters little in running wear. Clothing should keep you warm, fit relatively loosely, and feel invisible on the run.

you want. After shoes, of course, clothing is somewhat unimportant, although it should keep you warm, be relatively loose fitting, and feel invisible on the run. Anything that has a tendency to bind or chafe will only cause grief.

In her book *Women's Running*, Dr. Joan Ullyot writes, "for short runs—up to five miles—go ahead and use your comfortable old bermudas, blue jeans, or whatever. Elegance doesn't matter. The only objection to such garments is that they usually start chafing on longer runs. I and many of my friends who run from a gym with a swimming pool have adopted Speedo men's swim trunks—low cut nylon briefs, two-layered so you don't need underpants. Any soft cotton shorts are good and usually are cheaper than the fancy women's track briefs sold by specialty shops."

Nina Kuscsik says "women need a firm bra, not one of the flimsy all-elastic ones. That's especially true if you have large breasts. Otherwise they'll bounce and you'll always be waiting for them to come down before you take the next step." Dr. Ullyot says, " . . . comfort is the only consideration, and chafing is the problem to guard against. If you're small-chested enough to run comfortably without a bra, be happy. Starting somewhere around a 34-B cup, most women begin to bounce uncomfortably if they run braless. If you are large-bosomed, you can still run, but you need more support from the bra in order to be comfortable." Dr. Ullyot reacts strongly to the suggestion that jogging can produce "sagging breasts." "This is nonsense," she says. "Sagging breasts result usually from overdistention (with fat) which can stretch the skin and break elastic fibers. Bouncing will not break these fibers."

Special Problems

Most doctors agree that exercise during menstruation is not just tolerated but encouraged. If pain is experienced, any exercise that stimulates blood circulation and muscle tone in the abdominal area can help reduce it. It is not impossible that the fit body will better handle and cope with any discomfort that may accompany menstruation.

Pregnancy need not stop women from running. Many women run up through the final month of their pregnancy. Exercise can help strengthen the uterus and there should be no question that the well-conditioned body is more ready for childbearing than the one which is unfit. Dr. Ullyot cautions that you should run aerobically, using Coach Bowerman's talk test to assure that both the mother and baby are receiving adequate oxygen. She also warns against competition. Dr. Ullyot adds, "the only condition in which exercise should be avoided is 'cervical incompetence,' a dilated or weakened cervix, which can cause second trimester miscarriage. Some pregnant women," she continues, "avoid exercise for fear of inducing miscarriage or jarring the fetus loose. Physiologically, this is nonsense.

Endurance is the backbone of a jogging program. It would be trivial to write less of a program for a woman than for a man.

At all stages of pregnancy the fetus is well protected and cushioned by the amniotic fluid—like fish in an aquarium. Moving the container around does not disturb the floating fetus."

There is no real evidence that women are any more susceptible to injury than are men. Take care to warm up properly, to choose a suitable distance and terrain, and to, as Connie Manley suggests, learn to listen to your body. Aches and pains mean your body is reacting uneasily to the strain. Change the strain.

In Eugene, we know little about one of the most common complaints of women who begin jogging: Ridicule. Long ago the first groups of women started ambling slowly through the city's streets. Expect a few comments, but be reassured in the envy of those who wish they could undo centuries of cultural deprivation as you are doing. Running in groups lends instant support, as well as the advantages of safety in numbers. In urban environments, women joggers should be careful to avoid darkness and dismal places. Some women joggers carry a small can of the mace-like chemical used to slow down dogs. Some just move more quickly than their would-be pursuers.

You'll notice that we write no special running programs for women. We believe our jogging programs will fit runners of any reasonable state of physical condition, and any sex. Since endurance—not speed and strength—is the backbone of a jogging program, it would be frivolous to write less of a program for a woman than a man. When it comes to jogging, a woman's place is just about anywhere she wants it to be.

6

The First Step

As you think about those first steps out the front door, you might be wondering how I could possibly identify with the beginning jogger. Or one day develop programs for world-class distance runners and on another develop a program for someone who has never run before. After all, for 15 years the biggest part of my life was devoted to competitive running. In preparing for high school championships, collegiate championships, and finally for three Olympic Games, I ran competitively from age 15 to age 30. But, just as Arthur Lydiard's New Zealand athletes had discovered, I, too, did not want to quit being physically fit just because it was the time in my life to quit competition. It made no sense to go from winning the bronze medal at the Tokyo Olympics to an easy chair in front of the television set. I love running, I love being in good condition, and I firmly believe that one enjoys all phases of life more when fit.

So it is that I have been a jogger the last 13 years. I run regularly, not nearly as fast and as hard as I used to do, but enough to relax the tensions that come from coaching

Bill Dellinger, who has jogged for nearly 15 years, runs daily, often taking a few laps with one of the trackmen, like Matt Centrowitz.

and enough to keep reasonably fit. The five-minute mile I ran with ease as a 30-year-old has become a seven-minute mile at age 43. And, too, I have had a couple of serious injuries to my calf muscles, something I trace now to a lack of adequate stretching before I run. In each case, I had to start a walking program, then a program of walking 10 steps and running 10 steps, and so on, until I could jog continuously at a very slow pace for a mile. So, in a sense, I began with the rank beginners.

With my background in competitive racing and now as a coach of track and field combined with my love for jogging, I believe I can help you with a running program, whether it be for competitive racing or just for jogging to help promote relaxation, enjoyment, and fitness. I understand that many of you will want to be competitive once you begin to improve as a jogger. For many, it may be a first taste of competition. But, for others, jogging can be a time to get away from the competitive, cutthroat world of business. Many of my friends still compete on the Masters level for people 40 years and older. For many reasons, I no longer want to compete. I could compete in local road runs and probably do pretty well. But I choose to run simply for fitness and my own enjoyment. I suspect that a lot of you approach it with the same goals. Okay, how do you take the first step en route to 20 minutes in the target zone, that important span of time where your heart beat is beating 70 to 85 percent of its maximal rate and your cardiovascular system is strengthening significantly?

Remember that time and speed, of course, are relative. This is an important consideration in your common sense program as the years roll by. Just as I can accept that the five-minute mile I ran with ease is now a seven-minute mile, you, too, must understand your own limitations. Rather than be concerned with how fast you can run, I believe the jogger running for fitness, thus enjoyment, should be more concerned about reaching a prolonged period of time at which he or she is capable of running aerobically, or at a rate where you feel no undue strain and where your body is receiving an adequate supply of oxygen from your heart and lungs. Remember, if you are running so fast that you feel a heavy amount of strain on your body, or that you cannot talk to yourself or a companion, then you are running too fast.

We have selected 20 minutes as the period of time you are attempting to achieve in a beginning jogging program. It doesn't sound like much, and it isn't. But a 20-minute run on a Sunday afternoon in place of watching another of those professional football games on television can have quite an impact on both your lifestyle and general physical fitness.

Run at a pace so you feel no undue strain and so your body is receiving an adequate supply of oxygen.

There is nothing magic about 20 minutes, other than the fact that the National Heart Association recommends it as the minimum amount of daily exercise time needed to significantly improve your cardiovascular system. There are other reasons I selected it, however:

It is long enough to be a challenge and give a feeling of achievement after completion.

For a fresh mental outlook toward jogging, vary your running by changing the routes and terrain occasionally.

Everyone can afford to give themselves 20 minutes a day in the important quest for physical fitness.

We've designed this program to start at square one. It will take a beginner who has not been running—perhaps has never really run before—literally step-by-step toward his goal of running 20 minutes a day. Remember what we said about the gloomy claim that 90 percent of those who start running today won't be running a year from now. Slow and steady can win this race to physical fitness. Don't be in a hurry. The running may seem easy at the beginning—and it should be. We've designed it to keep enthusiasm up and pain down. As your fitness increases, so does the difficulty of the program. Gradually, you run farther and farther. The goal is both to be able to run continuously for 20 minutes and to do it with a feeling of fulfillment, achievement, and enjoyment.

It would be nice if every community had jogging trails available as we have in Eugene. It might be even more convenient if a measured 440-yard track were near your home for jogging. But since this is not always possible—and because a growing number of people disdain the confines of a track—our jogging program is based on a count system, not on distance measured on a track, as so many are. I mentioned earlier about the time I spent stationed at a remote radar site on the Olympic Peninsula in the state of Washington during some of the most important years of my competition. The nearest track was 80 miles away. In the place of a track, where I had always done the bulk of my training, I would run up and down the ocean beach counting strides to measure the distance I was covering. Each time my right foot would strike the ground, I would count one to myself. When I reached 10, I would put my thumb out. Upon reaching 10 the second time, I would put out my forefinger and so on until I had run for six fingers, 10 fingers, 12 fingers or whatever distance I wanted to cover. I estimated that six fingers was approximately 220 yards, 12 fingers a 440, or once around the track I didn't have, and so on. I used this system for nine months of training and ran a 4:05 mile the first time I stepped on a track the following spring. I went on that summer of 1958 to establish American records in the 1,500 meters, the two-mile, the three-mile, and the 5,000 meters.

We believe the count system can be adapted to any running environment, and to any stage of physical fitness. Indeed, we believe it is particularly suited for the beginning jogger. The very first day of our beginning program consists of jogging for 10 counts (or one finger)—counting each time the right foot hits the ground—alternated with walking for 20 counts (or two fingers). And this jogging-walking goes on for 20 minutes.

Immediately, you have devoted 20 minutes to exercise. Even though the beginning is far from strenuous, the discipline is there. You are alloting at least 20 minutes of time to exercise, be it 20 minutes right after you roll out of bed in the morning, or 20 minutes during the lunch hour, or 20 minutes after work.

You will notice that many of the principles we apply to the training of world-class distance runners are used in this beginning program. You mix jogging and walking the first day, and then just walk the second day, or Oregon's famous hard-easy approach. Toward the end of the ten-week program I attempted to make Tuesday, Thursday, and Saturday the hard days with Monday, Wednesday, and Friday the easy days.

Besides the principle of moderation, which the entire program is based upon, you must be aware of the principle of variation. For a fresh mental outlook toward jogging, vary your running occasionally by changing the terrain and routes. We have made the program adaptable to any location; you need to make it adaptable to your own level of physical fitness. You might be playing basketball once a week, or bicycling on Sunday, or swimming during the summer and find the beginning program too easy taken from step one. Using common sense, pick a week that looks well within reason and start there. Your body will tell you if the week you've picked is too demanding. Remember that it does no good to run anaerobically, and you can easily measure that with the talk test.

When you reach a point of being able to jog continuously for 20 minutes you have accomplished something few have. Be happy and have a feeling of accomplishment. Now the challenge becomes one of being consistent and reaching a state where running or jogging becomes a part of your life.

Here is a 10-week program for a beginning jogger.

EVENT: BEGINNING JOGGER

WEEK: #1

DATES:

DAY	WORKOUT	COMMENTS
M 1	Using Count System Jog 10 counts, right foot Walk 20 counts, right foot Continue for 20 minutes	Time permitting, easy stretching before and after run—refer to Chapter 4
Tu 2	20-minute walk	
W 3	Using Count System Jog 20 counts, right foot Walk 20 counts, right foot Continue for 20 minutes	

Th **4**	20-minute walk	
F **5**	Using Count System Jog 20 counts, right foot Walk 10 counts, right foot Continue for 20 minutes	
Sa **6**	20-minute walk	
Su **7**	Active rest	Could include cutting wood, swimming, bicycle riding, bowling, hiking, etc.

EVENT: BEGINNING JOGGER

WEEK: #2

DATES:

DAY	WORKOUT	COMMENTS
M 8	Using Count System Jog 20 counts Walk 20 counts Continue for 20 minutes	
Tu 9	(1) Walk 5 minutes (2) Jog 5 minutes using count system. Jog 50 counts, walk 50 counts (3) Walk 5 minutes (4) Jog 50 counts, walk 50 counts for 5 minutes	
W 10	Using Count System Jog 30 counts Walk 20 counts Continue for 20 minutes	

Th **11**	(1) Walk 5 minutes (2) Jog 50 counts, walk 50 counts for 5 minutes (3) Walk 5 minutes (4) Jog 50 counts, walk 50 counts for 5 minutes	
F **12**	Using Count System Jog 40 counts Walk 20 counts Continue for 20 minutes	
Sa **13**	(1) Walk 5 minutes (2) Jog 50 counts, walk 50 counts for 5 minutes (3) Walk 5 minutes (4) Jog 50 counts, walk 50 counts for 5 minutes	
Su **14**	Active rest	Could include cutting wood, swimming, bicycle riding, hiking, etc.

EVENT: BEGINNING JOGGER

WEEK: #3

DATES:

DAY	WORKOUT	COMMENTS
M 15	Using Count System Jog 30 counts Walk 20 counts Continue for 20 minutes	
Tu 16	(1) 5-minute brisk walk (2) Jog 50 counts, walk 40 counts—5 minutes (3) 5-minute brisk walk (4) Jog 50 counts, walk 40 counts—5 minutes	
W 17	Using Count System Jog 40 counts Walk 20 counts Continue for 20 minutes	

Th **18**	(1) 5-minute brisk walk (2) Jog 50 counts, walk 40 counts—5 minutes (3) 5-minute brisk walk (4) Jog 50 counts, walk 40 counts—5 minutes	
F **19**	Using Count System Jog 50 counts Walk 30 counts Continue for 20 minutes	
Sa **20**	(1) 5-minute brisk walk (2) Jog 50 counts, walk 40 counts—5 minutes (3) 5-minute brisk walk (4) Jog 50 counts, walk 40 counts—5 minutes	
Su **21**	Active rest	

EVENT: BEGINNING JOGGER

WEEK: #4

DATES:

DAY	WORKOUT	COMMENTS
M 22	Using Count System Jog 40 counts Walk 20 counts Continue for 20 minutes	
Tu 23	(1) 5-minute brisk walk (2) Jog 50 counts, 5 minutes—30-count rest (3) 5-minute brisk walk (4) Jog 50 counts, 5 minutes—30-count rest	
W 24	Using Count System Jog 50 counts Walk 20 counts Continue for 20 minutes	

Th 25	(1) 5-minute brisk walk (2) Jog 50 counts, 5 minutes—30-count rest (3) 5-minute brisk walk (4) Jog 50 counts, 5 minutes—30-count rest	
F 26	Using Count System Jog 60 counts Walk 20 counts Continue for 20 minutes	
Sa 27	(1) 5-minute brisk walk (2) Jog 50 counts, 5 minutes—30-count rest (3) 5-minute brisk walk (4) Jog 50 counts, 5 minutes—30-count rest	
Su 28	Active rest	

EVENT: BEGINNING JOGGING

WEEK: #5

DATES:

DAY	WORKOUT	COMMENTS
M 29	Using Count System Jog 50 counts Walk 20 counts Continue 20 minutes	
Tu 30	(1) 5-minute brisk walk (2) 5-minute easy jog (3) 5-minute brisk walk (4) 5-minute easy jog	
W 31	Using Count System Jog 60 counts Walk 20 counts Continue 20 minutes	

Th **32**	(1) 5-minute brisk walk (2) 5-minute easy jog (3) 5-minute brisk walk (4) 5-minute easy jog	
F **33**	Using Count System Jog 70 counts Walk 20 counts Continue for 20 minutes	
Sa **34**	(1) 5-minute brisk walk (2) 5-minute easy jog (3) 5-minute brisk walk (4) 5-minute easy jog	
Su **35**	Active rest	

EVENT: BEGINNING JOGGER

WEEK: #6

DATES:

DAY	WORKOUT	COMMENTS
M 36	Using Count System Jog 70 counts Walk 20 counts Continue for 20 minutes	
Tu 37	(1) 5-minute brisk walk (2) 5-minute jog at comfortable pace (3) 5-minute brisk walk (4) 5-minute jog at comfortable pace	
W 38	Using Count System Jog 80 counts Walk 20 counts Continue for 20 minutes	

Th **39**	(1) 5-minute walk, brisk pace (2) 5-minute jog, easy pace (3) 5-minute walk, brisk pace (4) 5-minute jog, easy pace	
F **40**	Using Count System Jog 90 counts Walk 20 counts Continue for 20 minutes	
Sa **41**	(1) 5-minute walk, brisk pace (2) 5-minute jog, easy pace (3) 5-minute walk, brisk pace (4) 5-minute jog, easy pace	
Su **42**	Active rest	

EVENT: BEGINNING JOGGER

WEEK: #7

DATES:

DAY	WORKOUT	COMMENTS
M 43	Using Count System Jog 90 counts Walk 20 counts Continue for 20 minutes	
Tu 44	(1) 5-minute walk (2) 5-minute jog (3) 5-minute walk (4) 5-minute jog	
W 45	Using Count System Jog 100 counts Walk 20 counts Continue for 20 minutes	

Th **46**	(1) 3-minute walk (2) 7-minute jog (3) 3-minute walk (4) 7-minute jog	
F **47**	Using Count System Jog 110 counts Walk 20 counts Continue for 20 minutes	
Sa **48**	(1) 5-minute walk (2) 10-minute jog (3) 5-minute walk	
Su **49**	Active rest	

EVENT: BEGINNING JOGGER

WEEK: #8

DATES:

DAY	WORKOUT	COMMENTS
M 50	Using Count System Jog 110 counts Walk 20 counts Continue for 20 minutes	
Tu 51	(1) 3-minute walk (2) 7-minute jog (3) 3-minute walk (4) 7-minute jog	
W 52	Using Count System Jog 120 counts Walk 20 counts Continue for 20 minutes	

Th **53**	(1) 5-minute walk (2) 10-minute jog (3) 5-minute walk	
F **54**	Using Count System Jog 130 counts Walk 20 counts Continue for 20 minutes	
Sa **55**	(1) 3-minute walk (2) 14-minute jog (3) 3-minute walk	
Su **56**	Active rest	

EVENT: BEGINNING JOGGER

WEEK: #9

DATES:

DAY	WORKOUT	COMMENTS
M 57	Using Count System Jog 130 counts Walk 20 counts Continue for 20 minutes	
Tu 58	(1) 5-minute walk (2) 10-minute jog (3) 5-minute walk	
W 59	Using Count System Jog 140 counts Walk 20 counts Continue for 20 minutes	

Th **60**	(1) 3-minute walk (2) 14-minute easy jog (3) 3-minute walk	
F **61**	Using Count System Jog 150 counts Walk 20 counts Continue for 20 minutes	
Sa **62**	20-minute easy jog	
Su **63**	Active rest	

EVENT: BEGINNING JOGGER

WEEK: #10

DATES:

DAY	WORKOUT	COMMENTS
M **64**	20-minute easy jog at a pace that feels comfortable	
Tu **65**	Using Count System Jog 150 counts fairly hard Jog 50 counts very easy Continue for 20 minutes	
W **66**	20-minute easy jog at a pace that feels comfortable Using Count System	

Th **67**	(1) 10 × 50 counts at good pace with a rest interval of 50 counts at very easy pace (2) Finish off the 20 minutes with easy jogging	
F **68**	20-minute easy jog at a pace that feels comfortable	
Sa **69**	Using Count System (1) 12 × 15 150 counts with a 50-count rest (2) Remainder of 20 minutes light jogging	
Su **70**	Active rest	

After you become able to jog continuously for 20 minutes, the next stage is to make running become a part of your life.

7

The Next Step

There is no lack of evidence that the world is full of people who want to run, and run not only against themselves, but against each other. Five thousand people toed the starting line (if that was possible) in the 1977 New York City marathon. Over 12,000 started the seven-mile Bay-to-Breakers run that same year in San Francisco. The Boston Marathon, of course, now has a qualifying time of three hours for its male entrants. We had almost 1,000 runners in Eugene for our six-mile Butte-to-Butte race through the city on a July 4th morning in 1977. Competitive running is not *the* thing in Eugene, not like it is in San Francisco or Boston. But, nevertheless, we believe that the greatest percentage of any jogging population is made up of people who have already been running 20 minutes a day or more for some time and wish to go a step farther.

Many of our joggers are people who, for one reason or another, never had the opportunity to get involved in competitive running at any level. They have never had the "taste" of competition to see what they could do in this

You will have the opportunity in road racing to get into low-key races like our Oregon Track Club fun runs.

situation. Having been a competitor and now being involved as a coach of competitors, I feel very strongly that there are some disciplines involved in preparation for competition that overlap as a positive influence on other phases of life.

Many of us need stimulation and reward to properly enjoy any activity. Exercise is no different. There may be a time when you want to put the body on display and test it in competition with others. Or just enjoy the companionship of others and the festival of competition. Road racing is one of the fastest growing sports in America today. You may have the opportunity to get into low-key fun runs organized by local running clubs. And, indeed, you may seek that kind of outlet. From there the sky and the Boston Marathon are the limit. In almost any running community there are highly organized road races for those who are no longer joggers, but are now called runners. If you want it, the opportunity will be there for you to run in races from two miles to marathon distance of over 26 miles.

Jogging easily for 20 minutes is one thing; running in a six-mile road run is quite another. Many joggers have no idea how to increase their distance once they get into the two or three-mile-a-day syndrome. Many may never want to compete but are simply seeking a systematic way to increase their mileage and involvement in jogging. That could well happen to you. While some are content to run two miles a day, many feel the need—both physically and psychologically—to go on.

If you have been running 20 minutes a day, you have been covering anywhere from 12 to 21 miles a week. In the program that follows, I will start with a 20-mile week and progress with weekly programs that will finally reach 80 miles a week. Most of our world-class runners don't run 80 miles a week. The program is there only for the very few who are serious about running a competitive age-group marathon.

I believe that anyone running a 20-mile week program is fit enough to run in a six-mile road race. He will run better, however, if he is on a 30- or 40-mile-a-week program. In the same vein, a runner doing the 40- or 50-mile program can probably make it through a marathon, but the performance will be better and the stress less if he is running the 60-mile program.

In increasing your mileage, you should stay on each step for at least four weeks. At Oregon, not only do we use the hard day, easy day principle, but we go a step further with a hard week followed by an easy week. I would recom-

Using the Fartlek ("speed play") system of running, you will learn to make accelerations during your run.

mend the same procedure on this program. If you are running a 30-mile week, come back with a 20-mile week. When you have moved up to 40 miles a week alternate it with a 30-mile week and so on.

You will notice in this training program that we are using the basis of the famous Holmer Fartlek System. The Swedes call it "speed play." Basically, it is a short span of interval work during a cross-country–type run. We will call it accelerations. In your very first workout in the 20-mile program, you will notice that it calls for 10 accelerated runs of approximately 100 yards during the two-mile run. Running at a comfortable pace for the two miles, you accelerate to a point which is no longer comfortable and you know you couldn't sustain for the entire run. The distance need not be exactly 100 yards, and you might grow to know it as the distance between telephone poles.

The next day consists of a four-mile run at steady pace. You are to time that run, and attempt to run the four miles faster in each of the next four weeks. This is not an all-out run but a steady pace of 70 to 80 percent of your best effort. The third day, a light day, consists of a very easy three-mile run at a comfortable pace. Remember through all of this that you are training, not straining. If the program is too hard, drop back. Or modify it to suit your needs. Your body will tell you what you can handle. For your Saturday run in the 20-mile week, you might think of running the "easy" mile at between seven and eight-minute pace, and the hard mile between six and seven-minute pace. But those are only suggestions.

The Marathon

We realize the incredible appetite among runners to make it through a marathon. This will not come without much training and some stress. I know of no way of running that distance without some stress.

You should probably look at a six-month program in

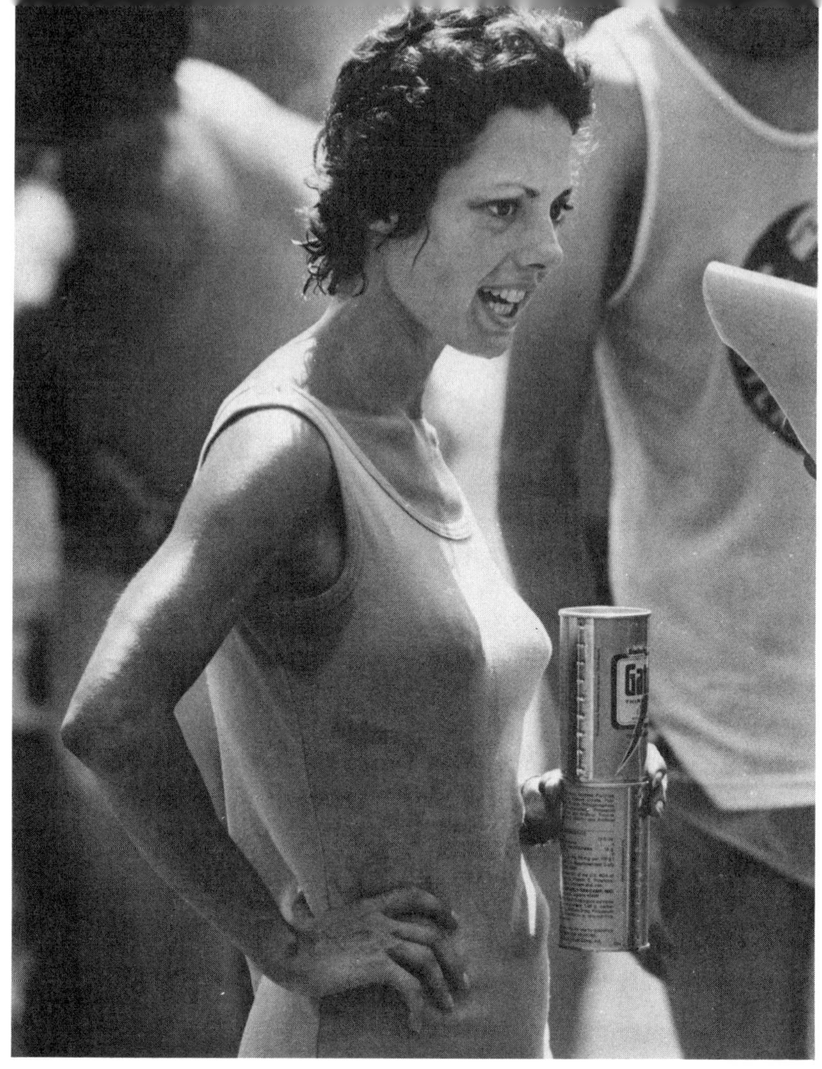

A marathon finisher is at least 15 percent dehydrated. Drink during a run, and especially after you've finished.

preparation for a marathon, depending, of course, on your present state of fitness. I would recommend that you get in at least one 60-mile week. You will notice, however, that the longest run in the 60-mile week covers only 12 miles. To be consistent with our belief in callusing a runner to a certain distance, I think it is necessary to modify the 50-

or 60-mile week to include either a 15-mile run or simply two hours of easy running to physically and mentally condition yourself to the marathon distance.

In running your first marathon, we should all remember the Greek who first covered the distance during the battle of Marathon—and died. Heat stroke, dehydration, heart problems, and a multitude of orthopedic problems await the unprepared marathoner.

During a recent marathon held in Portland, the official program carried a "Warning to Beginners." Included in the recommendations by Dr. James S. Puterbaugh were these:

—Remember, no one finishes a marathon who is not at least fifteen percent dehydrated. The fluid stands are an absolute medical and athletic necessity. Don't bypass them. Don't take a swallow and run. Stand there and drink a full glass or more—whatever you can drink comfortably.

—Run the marathon in the shoes you wore for training—not the new racing flats you've been waiting to use.

—Underdress for the weather; you will be plenty warm shortly into the run.

—Don't stop at the finish line. Walk for about ten minutes.

—Drink fluids immediately after the race.

—If you hurt something during the run—a knee, Achilles tendon, ankle or foot—Stop. You will prevent serious injury this way.

—Run at a pace which allows you to talk comfortably. Try to hold the same pace the entire race.

We believe that our experiences at Oregon—our development of the hard-day, easy-day approach, our use of Fartlek, our general philosophy of fewer miles, not more miles, can be especially useful to the jogger who wants to get in shape for longer, more competitive runs. In using the following programs, remember the principles of moderation, adaptability, variation, progression and callusing. And remember to have fun.

EVENT: THE NEXT STEP

WEEK: Step #1

DATES:

20-MILE WEEK

DAY	WORKOUT	COMMENTS
M 1	2-mile run. During this run do 10 acceleration runs of approximately 100 yards.	Make use of the count system in the beginning program for the accelerations
Tu 2	4-mile run at steady pace. Each week for the next 4 weeks, attempt to run faster on this run.	Time it! Run 70–80 percent of top effort
W 3	3-mile run at easy, comfortable pace you can handle without undue stress.	

Th **4**	2-mile run. During this run do 8 accelerations of approximately 200 yards each.	
F **5**	2 miles at very easy jog.	On grass if possible!
Sa **6**	5-mile run. Alternate running one mile hard, the next easy. If you cannot measure the distance, use a time span such as 5 minutes easy, 5 minutes hard for 25 minutes.	
Su **7**	2-mile run at comfortable pace.	

EVENT: THE NEXT STEP

WEEK: Step #2

DATES:

30-MILE WEEK

DAY	WORKOUT	COMMENTS
M 1	4-mile run varying the pace. During the run do 8 accelerations of 1 minute or approximately 300 yards.	
Tu 2	6-mile run at a steady pace. Each week attempt to run this 6 miles a little faster.	
W 3	3-mile run at a pace that feels easy and relaxing to you.	

Th **4**	5-mile run. If hills are available, run hard up a few hills of approximately 200 yards in length. If no hills, do 12 accelerations of approximately 200 yards.	
F **5**	2 miles of very easy running on grass, if possible.	
Sa **6**	6-mile run, running alternately a hard mile followed by an easy mile. Time yourself if necessary!	
Su **7**	4-mile run at comfortable pace.	

EVENT: THE NEXT STEP

WEEK: Step #3

DATES:

40-MILE WEEK

DAY	WORKOUT	COMMENTS
M **1**	5-mile run. During the run do 6 accelerations of 2 minutes or approximately 600 yards.	
Tu **2**	8-mile run. Start easy and make each mile a little faster than the last.	
W **3**	4-mile run at easy, comfortable pace.	

Th **4**	7-mile run. During this run, attempt 12–20 accelerations of approximately 200 yards or 35–40 seconds.	
F **5**	3 miles of easy grass run or other soft surface.	
Sa **6**	8-mile run. Run 2 miles easy, 2 miles hard, 2 miles easy, 2 miles hard.	
Su **7**	5-mile comfortable run.	

EVENT: THE NEXT STEP

WEEK: Step #4

DATES:

50-MILE WEEK

DAY	WORKOUT	COMMENTS
M 1	7-mile varied run. Do 6 accelerations of 3 minutes or approximately 1,000 yards.	
Tu 2	10-mile run. Start easy and increase speed over every 2 miles.	
W 3	5-mile comfortable run.	

Th **4**	9-mile run with 24 accelerations of approximately 200 yards.	
F **5**	4-mile easy run.	
Sa **6**	10-mile run. 3rd, 6th, and 9th miles at hard pace, miles in between should be nice and comfortable.	
Su **7**	6-mile easy run.	

EVENT: THE NEXT STEP

WEEK: Step #5

DATES:

60-MILE WEEK

DAY	WORKOUT	COMMENTS
M 1	8-mile run. During this, run 8 accelerations of 3 minutes or approximately 1,000 yards.	
Tu 2	12-mile run at steady, comfortable pace.	
W 3	6-mile run, very easy.	

Th **4**	10-mile run. Do 24 accelerations of approximately 200 yards or 35 seconds.	
F **5**	5 miles of very easy jogging.	
Sa **6**	12-mile run in the following manner: easy mile medium-pace mile hard-pace mile } Repeat four times for the 12 miles	
Su **7**	7 miles at comfortable pace.	

EVENT: THE NEXT STEP

WEEK: Step #6

DATES:

70-MILE WEEK

DAY	WORKOUT	COMMENTS
M 1	9-mile run. Do 8 accelerations of 3 minutes or approximately 1,000 yards.	
Tu 2	A.M.—2-mile easy jog. P.M.—12-mile run at steady, comfortable pace.	
W 3	7-mile easy run.	

Th **4**	A.M.—2-mile easy run. P.M.—10-mile run with 16 × approximately 200 yards.	
F **5**	6-mile easy run.	
Sa **6**	A.M.—12-mile run, alternating hard mile, easy mile. P.M.—2-mile easy jog.	
Su **7**	8-mile comfortable run.	

EVENT: THE NEXT STEP

WEEK: Step #7

DATES:

80-MILE WEEK

DAY	WORKOUT	COMMENTS
M 1	10-mile run with varied pace as to how you feel.	
Tu 2	A.M.—4-mile easy run. P.M.—12-mile run at steady pace you can carry throughout.	
W 3	8-mile easy run.	

Th **4**	A.M.—4-mile easy run. P.M.—10-mile run with 16–24 × approximately 200 yards of accelerated runs.	
F **5**	6 miles of light jogging.	
Sa **6**	A.M.—10-mile run at steady pace. P.M.—5-mile run at relaxing pace.	
Su **7**	10-mile easy run.	

8

Beyond Jogging

Although we realize running should be fun and relaxing, we also realize there are those individuals who have a desire to prepare themselves for competitions, either against other runners, or against themselves.

Perhaps you've run in monthly Masters programs for people over 40 years of age. Perhaps you run the mile in around seven minutes. You believe you are capable of running faster, and are willing to put in the necessary extra work to improve. What do you do?

We believe it is possible for you to use the programs we have developed at Oregon to develop a flock of world-class distance runners in the past two decades. The running program I used for Steve Prefontaine can be the same program you can use to improve your mile time because of something we call date-pace, goal-pace.

The date-pace, goal-pace method allows us flexibility in coaching our runners at Oregon. It also allows the flexibility of including you, no matter what your speed and experience, in the same program.

You would not consider teaching math to a group of

Competition can spice your jogging program.

people without first testing them to determine their knowledge of the subject. At Oregon, we test all of our runners during the first couple of weeks of school over their distance at a pace they can handle comfortably, thus establishing their date-pace. If you comfortably ran a six-minute mile, for example, then your date-pace would be 90 seconds for a 440.

Goal-pace, then, is a subjective evaluation of yourself by yourself or with the help of a coach in establishing the goal you wish to achieve. Once previous times have been established, your desire and the amount of time you wish to dedicate to the pursuit of this goal should be used, along with common sense, in setting the goal-pace. Make it tough but be realistic. You will progress obviously from workouts based on your date pace to those of goal pace.

Much of our philosophy in developing this program came from a 1960 study of Oregon runners. They were divided into three groups with one group put on a program of straight interval workouts done on the track, the second group on a Fartlek program of varied runs or speed play, and the third group on a combination of Fartlek training and intervals. By the end of the school year, the following conclusions were made:

The runners on straight interval work had the best early test efforts; by the end of the year, however, they had fallen behind the other two sections. As a group, they had the most injuries.

The runners on the Fartlek program were the most injury-free group, peaked the latest, but never reached their goals.

The runners on the program combining interval training with Fartlek training obtained the best overall results, hitting their peak when the time was right and achieving a higher level than the other two sections.

Another study about the same time indicated the desirability of our hard day, easy day pattern. The runner who had too many hard days without giving the body an opportunity to replenish destroyed and worn-out cells would eventually break down.

As a direct result of these two studies, the Oregon program is a blend of interval training based on date-and-goal pace, Fartlek training—both steady and varied, and, for the most part, a hard day followed by one or two easy days.

Fartlek is a Swedish term meaning "speed play." Dur-

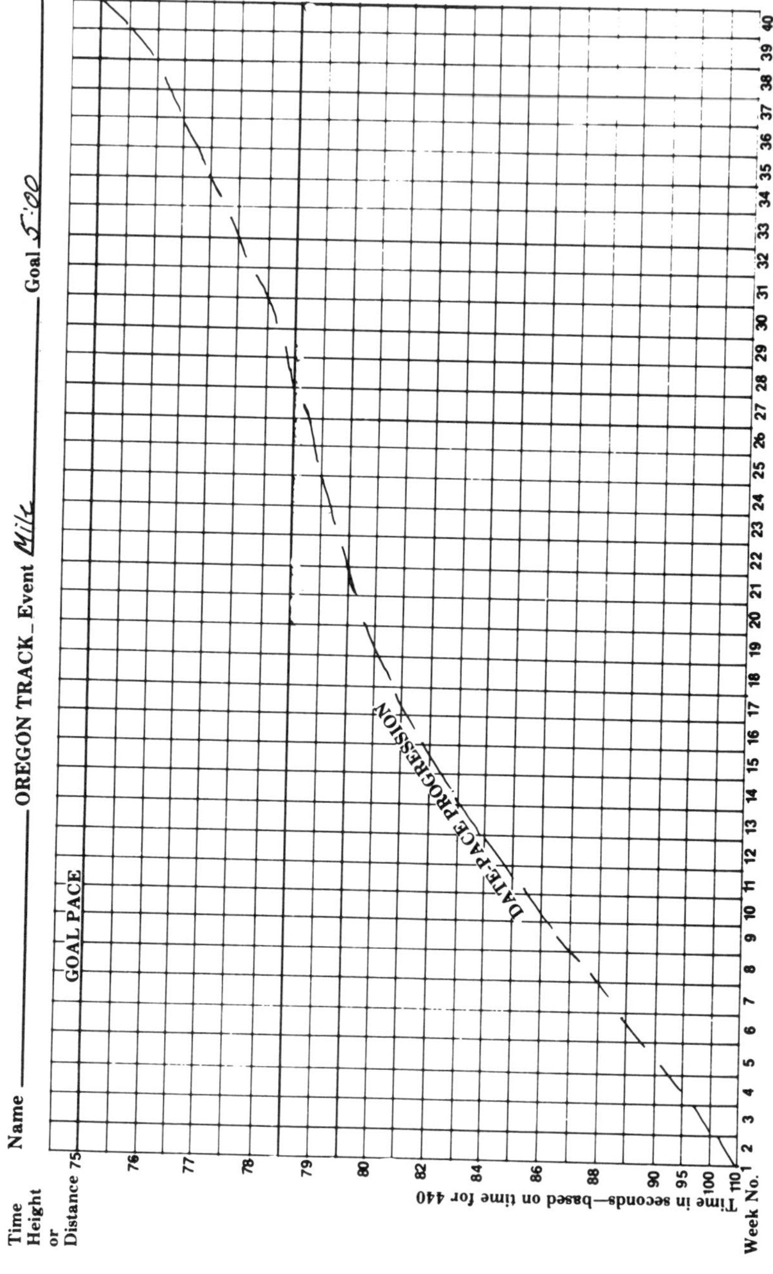

Name
OREGON TRACK Event Mile
Goal 5:00
GOAL PACE
DATE-PACE PROGRESSION
Time Height or Distance
75 76 77 78 79 80 82 84 86 88 90 95 100 110
Time in seconds—based on time for 440
Week No.
1 2 3 4 5 6 7 8 9 10 11 12 13 14 15 16 17 18 19 20 21 22 23 24 25 26 27 28 29 30 31 32 33 34 35 36 37 38 39 40

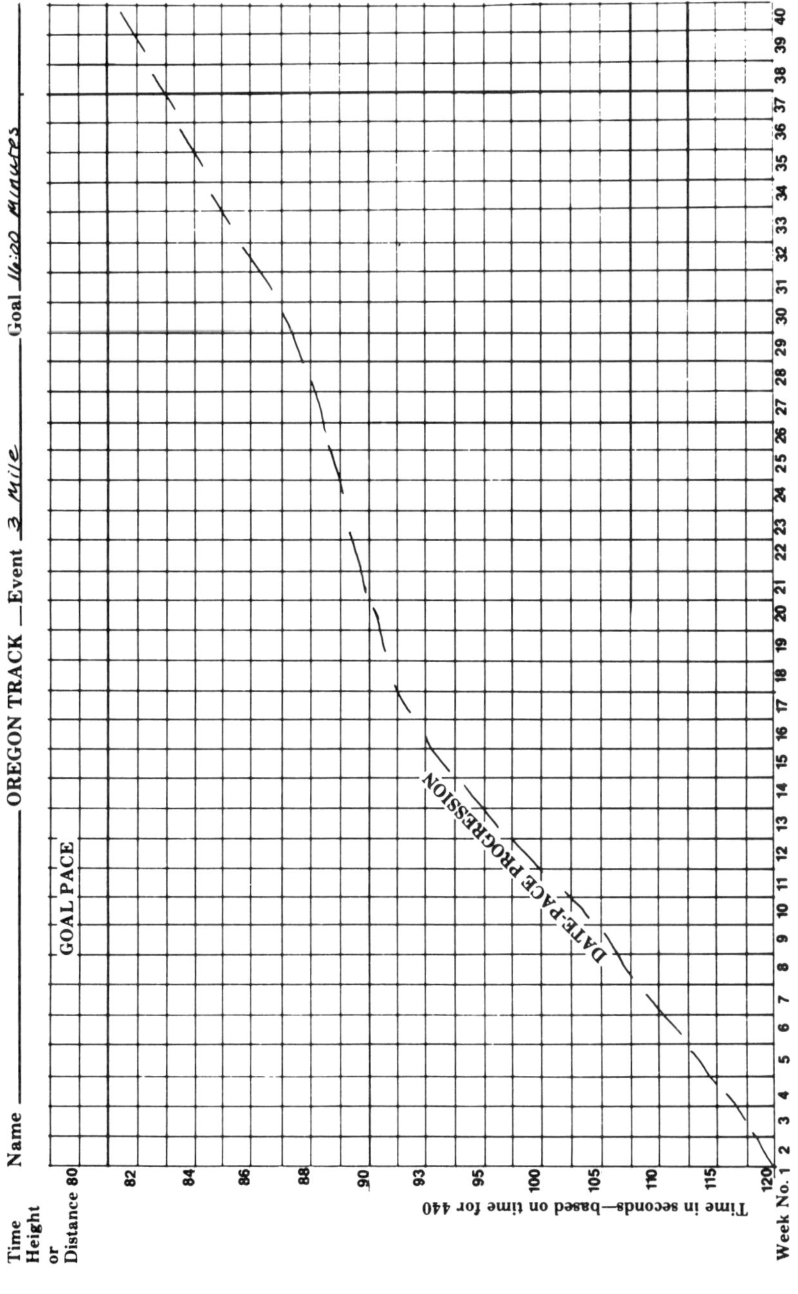
Name
OREGON TRACK
Event 3 mile
Goal 16:00 minutes
Time Height or Distance
Time in seconds—based on time for 440
Week No.
GOAL PACE
DATE-PACE PROGRESSION
80
82
84
86
88
90
93
95
100
105
110
115
120
1
2
3
4
5
6
7
8
9
10
11
12
13
14
15
16
17
18
19
20
21
22
23
24
25
26
27
28
29
30
31
32
33
34
35
36
37
38
39
40

ing the late 1930s into the middle 1940s, the world running scene was dominated by the Swedes. Such great runners as Henry Kalarne, Gundar Haag, Arne Andersen, and Lennart Strand were using a system of training devised by Gosta Holmer that involved delightfully exhausting 90- to 120-minute wind sprints through the silent and nearly endless pine forests of Sweden. With the success of the Swedes, many coaches adopted this training method; and it became known as the Holmer Fartlek System.

During the 1960s and 1970s, Arthur Lydiard developed many world-class runners. As a means of developing a strong foundation for their short span of interval training before the competitive season, Lydiard would send his runners on long runs, usually on roads, that were timed and run at a steady but relatively fast pace. Thus the term Lydiard Fartlek evolved. Many Americans interpret Fartlek training as any running that is not accomplished on the track. At Oregon, our program is more specific. We specify if one is to go on a varied Fartlek run, or a steady Fartlek run. We feel there are advantages to both systems and attempt to adapt them to our situation for best results.

You will notice that we talk about easy runs in the following programs. We ask our runners to cover a minimum of miles at a pace at which they feel relaxed and can enjoy. It is a run on "how you feel." If one is particularly tired, it may be no more than a 10-minute jog, followed by easy stretching.

The running program presented is broken down into a 21-day pattern during the off-season, a 14-day pattern for the competitive season and a 10-day pattern for the major or final competition. The first program is aimed at the runner who wishes to compete or improve at distances from the 880 through the three-mile. The second section is aimed at the competitor who wishes to compete at distances of three miles or longer.

The program will almost immediately begin exposing the runner to some goal-pace work, covering as much as one times your racing distance at short intervals you can handle. In the same workout, you may also cover two to four times your racing distance using longer intervals at date-pace for volume. As the program progresses, the goal-pace intervals will get longer and the date-pace intervals shorter.

Constant evaluation is necessary, especially in the off-season, so that adjustments in the program can be made. At Oregon, during the noncompetitive season we will work on a 21-day pattern, evaluating progress at the end of the 21 days by a date-pace testing over the full distance. Not only is progression being evaluated, but the runner is becoming callused to this distance at which he will compete during the competitive season.

To begin with, obviously, you will want to run a comfortable date-pace at the distance at which you want to compete. Then you will set a reasonable goal at that distance and compute your goal-pace. After 21 days on the program during the off-season you will rerun the new distance to set a new date-pace, which subsequently will make the workouts more difficult as you repeat the 21-day program.

It should be noted that a morning run is not included in this program. If you have the time, a 20-minute run each morning is recommended. To be competitive at an international level, it would be a necessity.

But to run well in the summer's jogger's mile it is not. That is the beauty of our running program. It helped Steve Prefontaine to every American distance record, and it can help you reach your potential as a distance runner—whatever that might be.

There is no question that the University of Oregon is producing America's finest stable of distance runners. This will give you an idea why.

EVENT: MILE

WEEK: #1

DATES:

21-DAY OFF-SEASON PERIOD

DAY	WORKOUT	COMMENTS
M 1	30–40 minutes varied Fartlek run, 8–12 times approximate 200-yard spurts during run.	It is assumed you have given yourself a date-pace test effort before starting this program. A goal-pace has also been set for you.
Tu 2	(1) 4–6 × 880 at date-pace with a 400 very easy jog between each 880. (2) 20 minutes of easy running.	
W 3	30–40 minutes of steady running at a comfortable pace.	

Th **4**	(1) 16 × 110 at goal-pace for mile. Each 220 jog between 110. (2) 20 minutes of easy running.	In all interval work, a warmup is recommended before starting the intervals!
F **5**	20–40 minutes of easy running.	Should include: (1) 10–15 minutes easy jogging. (2) Easy stretching. (3) 2–3 strides of approx. 110 yards making each a little faster.
Sa **6**	7–10 mile run. Start easy and gradually increase the tempo to finish with a hard pace you could not hold throughout the total run.	
Su **7**	20–40 minute easy run.	

EVENT: MILE

WEEK: #2

DATES:

21-DAY OFF-SEASON PERIOD

DAY	WORKOUT	COMMENTS
M 8	30–40 minutes varied Fartlek run. 20 × approximately 100 yards during this run at near full speed.	
Tu 9	5–7 mile run at a hard pace. Preferably have a measured course and time yourself over it.	
W 10	Easy run of 20–40 minutes depending on how you feel.	

Th 11	(1) 10 × 165 yards at mile-goal pace with a 200-yard rest between each. (2) 20 minutes of easy running.	
F 12	Easy run depending on how you feel.	
Sa 13	(1) 4 × ¾ mile at ¾ effort of date-pace. Jog an easy 880 between each ¾. (2) Easy run.	Refer to date-pace effort chart at end of chapter.
Su 14	7–10 miles of very easy running.	

EVENT: MILE

WEEK: #3

DATES:

21-DAY OFF-SEASON PERIOD

DAY	WORKOUT	COMMENTS
M 15	30–40 minute varied Fartlek run with 8–12 × approximately 200 yards during this run.	
Tu 16	(1) 6 × 330 at goal pace for mile with a 330 rest between each. (2) 5-mile run at comfortable pace.	
W 17	20–40 minute easy run depending on how you feel.	

Th 18	(1) 1 × 660 at goal-pace for mile; jog easy 880 for recovery. (2) 5 × 220 at date-pace for mile with a 220 rest between each. (3) Easy run of 20 minutes.	
F 19	20–40 minutes of easy running.	
Sa 20	(1) Mile test effort at ¾ effort of date-pace accelerating the last 440 to full date-pace. (2) 5-mile easy run.	Refer to date-pace effort chart at end of chapter. Record results of test on profile chart.
Su 21	7–10 miles very easy running.	

EVENT: MILE

WEEK: #1

DATES:

10-DAY PREPARATION FOR MAJOR COMPETITION

DAY	WORKOUT	COMMENTS
Th **1**	(1) 2½ laps at goal-pace for mile; 660 easy jog. (2) 1½ laps at goal-pace for mile. (3) 20-minute grass run.	
F **2**	30-minute grass run at easy pace.	
Sa **3**	(1) 2-mile on track at ½ effort date-pace for mile. (2) 30-minute run at comfortable pace.	

Su **4**	10-mile run at comfortable pace.	
M **5**	40-minute varied Fartlek run.	
Tu **6**	(1) 880 at full effort. (2) 20-minute grass run. (3) 3 × 330 goal-pace for mile, 220 jog between.	
W **7**	30–40 minute grass run at comfortable pace.	

EVENT: MILE

WEEK:

DATES:

10-DAY PREPARATION FOR MAJOR COMPETITION

DAY	WORKOUT	COMMENTS
M **8**	(1) 3 × 440 goal-pace for mile with a 220 jog between. (2) 20-minute grass run.	
Tu **9**	30-minute easy running on grass or soft surface.	
W **10**	Competition.	

You may want to train seriously for age-group competitions.

EVENT: MILE

WEEK: #1

DATES:

14-DAY COMPETITIVE PERIOD

DAY	WORKOUT	COMMENTS
M 1	(1) 30-minute varied Fartlek run. (2) 6 × 220 at goal-pace for mile with a 30-second rest interval.	
Tu 2	(1) 3 × 880 at goal-pace with 660 jog between each. (2) 2 × mile at ¾ effort date-pace. 880 jog between. (2) Light grass run 15 minutes.	
W 3	30–40 minute run at comfortable pace.	

Th **4**	(1) 6 × 330 yards at goal pace for mile, 220 jog between each. (2) 20-minute steady run at comfortable pace. (3) 4 × 110 goal-pace for 880; 110 jog between.	
F **5**	20–30 minute easy grass run.	
Sa **6**	Compete. If you have the opportunity, compete at an under distance. Perhaps an 880!	
Su **7**	7–10 mile run at easy, comfortable pace.	

EVENT: MILE

WEEK: #2

DATES:

14-DAY COMPETITIVE PERIOD

DAY	WORKOUT	COMMENTS
M 8	(1) 4 × 220 goal-pace for mile with 30-second rest interval. (2) 30-minute steady run at comfortable pace. (3) 4 × 220 goal-pace for mile; 30-second rest interval.	
Tu 9	(1) 440—660—440—220 at goal-pace for a mile. 330 jog between each. (2) 3 × 880 at ¾ effort date-pace for mile; 440 jog between. (3) Easy grass jog for 10 minutes.	
W 10	30-minute easy run.	

Th 11	(1) 3 × 440—1–2 seconds faster than goal-pace for mile; 440 jog between. (2) 20-minute easy grass run.	
F 12	15–25 minutc casy grass run.	
Sa 13	Compete. Attempt to compete in a mile or 2 mile.	
Su 14	7–10 mile easy run.	

EVENT: 3–6 MILE

WEEK: #1

DATES:

21-DAY OFF-SEASON PATTERN

DAY	WORKOUT	COMMENTS
M 1	40–60 minutes of varied pace running.	
Tu 2	(1) 3 × 440 goal-pace with 220 jog between. (2) 3 × ¾ mile at date-pace with 660 jog between. (3) Easy grass run for 10 minutes.	
W 3	30–40 minutes of easy running.	

Th 4	40 minutes of varied pace running. During this run 8–12 × approximate 300 yards of accelerated run.	
F 5	20–40 minutes of easy running.	
Sa 6	10-mile run over a measured course. Run at ½ effort date-pace for 6 miles.	Refer to effort chart at end of chapter.
Su 7	8–12 mile run at comfortable pace.	

EVENT: 3–6 MILE

WEEK: #2

DATES:

21-DAY OFF-SEASON PATTERN

DAY	WORKOUT	COMMENTS
M 8	40–60 minutes of varied pace running. During this run do 16–24 accelerated approximately 100 yards with 2 minutes of easy running between.	
Tu 9	(1) 4 × 440 at goal-pace for mile with 440 jog between. (2) 30 minutes of easy running.	Even though your primary goal is for a 3 or 6 mile, select a goal-pace for 1 mile as this will be a basis for speed work.
W 10	30–40 minutes of easy running at steady pace.	

Th 11	(1) Timed 2-mile at ¾ effort date-pace for 6-mile. (2) 5 × 330 starting at date-pace for 6-mile and making each faster, ending with goal-pace for mile.	
F 12	20 40 minute easy jogging.	
Sa 13	(1) 4–6 × 1 mile at ¾ effort date-pace for 3-mile; jog an 880 between each mile. (2) 10–15 minute easy jogging.	
Su 14	7–12 mile run at comfortable pace.	

EVENT: 3–6 MILE

WEEK: #3

DATES:

21-DAY OFF-SEASON PATTERN

DAY	WORKOUT	COMMENTS
M 15	40–60 minute varied run. Add several accelerations of varying distances depending upon how you feel.	
Tu 16	(1) 5 × 2½ laps at date-pace for 3-mile with a 440 jog between. (2) Light jog for 10 minutes.	
W 17	30–40 minutes of comfortable running at a steady pace.	

Th 18	(1) 440—660—440—220 at goal-pace for a mile with a 440 rest between each. (2) 20 minutes of easy running.	
F 19	20–40 minutes easy running.	
Sa 20	(1) Test effort for 3-mile. Depending upon conditions, attempt to run at ¾ effort date-pace. (2) 20-minute easy run.	
Su 21	40-minute easy run.	

EVENT: 3–6 MILE

WEEK: #1

DATES:

14-DAY COMPETITIVE PATTERN

DAY	WORKOUT	COMMENTS
M 1	(1) 40-minute varied Fartlek run. (2) 8 × 220 at goal-pace for mile with a 30–45 second rest to complete the run.	
Tu 2	(1) 6 × 880 at goal-pace for a 3-mile with a 440–660 jog between. (2) 20-minute easy grass run.	
W 3	40-minute steady run at a comfortable pace.	

Th 4	(1) 5 × 330 yards at goal-pace for a mile with a 220 jog between. (2) 30-minute grass run at easy pace.	
F 5	20–40 minutes of grass running.	
Sa 6	Compete. Attempt to run under or over your primary event. One mile or 6 miles if your event is the 3-mile.	
Su 7	Easy run of 40 minutes.	

EVENT: 3–6 MILE

WEEK: #2

DATES:

14-DAY COMPETITIVE PATTERN

DAY	WORKOUT	COMMENTS
M 8	(1) 40-minute varied Fartlek run. (2) 8–12 × 220 at goal-pace for a mile with a 30-second rest at completion of run.	
Tu 9	(1) 2½ laps, 1½ laps at goal-pace for a mile with an 880 jog between. (2) 2 miles at ¾ effort date-pace for a 3-mile. (3) Easy grass run 10–20 minutes.	
W 10	30–40 minute steady run at comfortable pace.	

Th **11**	(1) 3 × 440 goal-pace for mile with a 330 jog between. (2) 20-minute grass run. (3) 3 × 330 at goal-pace for 3-mile, 110 jog between.	
F **12**	20–40 minute easy grass run.	
Sa **13**	3-mile competition.	
Su **14**	8–12 miles at easy pace.	

EVENT: 3–6 MILE

WEEK: #1

DATES:

10-DAY PREPARATION FOR MAJOR COMPETITION

DAY	WORKOUT	COMMENTS
Th **15**	(1) 4 × ¾ mile at goal-pace for 3-mile with an 880 jog between each. (2) 3 × 1 mile at date-pace for 6-mile with an 880 jog between each.	
F **16**	20–40 minutes of easy running.	
Sa **17**	8-mile run at medium pace.	

Su **4**	8–12 mile easy run.	
M **5**	40-minute varied run.	
Tu **6**	(1) 1 × ¾ mile at goal-pace for mile. (2) 30-minute easy run. (3) 3 × 330 at goal pace for 3-mile with 220 jog between.	
W **7**	30–40 minute steady run at comfortable pace.	

EVENT: 3–6 MILE

WEEK: #2

DATES:

10-DAY PREPARATION FOR MAJOR COMPETITION

DAY	WORKOUT	COMMENTS
Th 8	4 miles at ½ effort date-pace for 3- or 6-mile.	
F 9	20–30 minutes easy grass run.	
Sa 10	Competition for 3- or 6-mile.	

DATE-PACE EFFORT CHART

Mile Time	440 Full Effort	¾ Effort	½ Effort
4:00	60 seconds	62–64 seconds	65–68 seconds
4:04	61	63–65	66–69
4:08	62	64–66	67–70
4:12	63	65–67	68–71
4:16	64	66–68	69–72
4:20	65	67–69	70–73
4:24	66	68–70	71–74
4:28	67	69–71	72–75
4:32	68	70–72	73–76
4:36	69	71–73	74–77
4:40	70	72–74	75–78
4:44	71	73–75	76–79
4:48	72	74–76	77–80
4:52	73	75–77	78–81
4:56	74	76–78	79–82
5:00	75	77–79	80–83
5:04	76	78–80	81–84
5:08	77	79–81	82–85
5:12	78	80–82	83–86
5:16	79	81–83	84–87
5:20	80	82–84	85–88
5:24	81	83–85	86–89
5:28	82	84–86	87–90
5:32	83	85–87	88–91
5:36	84	86–88	89–92
5:40	85	87–89	90–93
5:44	86	88–90	91–94
5:48	87	89–91	92–95
5:52	88	90–92	93–96
5:56	89	91–93	94–97
6:00	90	92–94	95–98

9

The Jogging Environment

A Disneyland for joggers? A Mecca for the motivated? Streets paved with sweat, Acrylic warmup suits, and $30 running shoes? What is Eugene, Oregon, all about? What made the mayor run a marathon and an estimated 10,000 of the citizenry run their way to physical fitness? Bill Bowerman, who is most to blame, said the running craze was due to the "chromosomes in the local cabbage."

Bowerman meant he couldn't explain the phenomenon, although there is no question that the area's mild, moist climate and its hero worship of track stars such as Dyrol Burleson, Jim Grelle and the late Steve Prefontaine came together with Bowerman's revelation that running at slow pace for a relatively long time can do wonders for your physical and mental well-being. He even went so far as to conclude that runners made better lovers.

It is now 1978. Prefontaine is dead, Bowerman has retired and yet there are more runners than ever in Eugene, although the city pales as a competitive distance running center to San Francisco and Boston, for example. Which we think is a positive sign.

"As far as road racing goes," says Jon Anderson, son of the mayor and winner of the 1973 Boston Marathon, "the two pockets of great distance running in this country are the San Francisco Bay Area and New England. Eugene just doesn't rate very high as far as lots of people being involved in competitive running. We are more of a jogging population content to run two, three, four or five miles a day. Some people never get involved in a race."

The Oregonian, we think, is more interested in physical fitness than announcing that he finished the famous Bay-to-Breakers grind in San Francisco. Even though the number of joggers has increased steadily in Eugene, as elsewhere, there are no more people in the few races we have than there were five years ago. "People here run as a supplement to their real recreational activity," said Jon Anderson. Roscoe Divine, himself a former sub-four-minute miler who now feels good just jogging five miles a day, five times a week, explains his motivation: "The main reason I jog, outside of clearing my head, is to allow myself to do other things. My passion is cross-country skiing."

Without mass numbers of people entering competitions, it is difficult to measure the extent of recreational running in Eugene. Geoff Hollister, a former Oregon runner and now an executive with the Oregon-based Nike Shoe Company, says he is convinced Eugene has the highest concentration of joggers per capita in the country. He says he's heard the figure put at two out of every three people, but he agrees that there are at least 10,000 of the city's 100,000 citizens pounding the streets and trails. "The climate, the environment, the whole attitude of people around here make it a good place to run," he said.

Pat Holleran, a fine runner for Notre Dame, annually visits Eugene for training and a bit of motivation. And shares his feelings with members of the Oregon Track Club through its monthly newsletter. "It was," wrote Holleran, "through reading about Steve Prefontaine that myself and others first came to be interested in the town

Eugene's jogging environment is a pleasant one: mild weather, scenic paths, and trails designed with the runner in mind.

and in this state. It had sounded so incredible—a town where a runner was the big sports hero and where running was not considered abnormal behavior. When coupled with the unequaled beauty of the state, the whole place became somewhat of a utopia to the runner and/or the environmental freak. I can never remember going for a run in Eugene and not seeing another runner. In South Bend, Indiana, unless I'm with the Notre Dame cross-country team, it's difficult to remember ever seeing another runner, even in these days of the 'jogging chic.' It's easier to run here with the gentle weather, the hills, the beauty, and the support of so many other runners."

More than weather and facilities, however, is the importance of attitude. It is entirely acceptable to run two miles to the grocery store, walk in with sweat dripping from your forehead and pick up a quart of yogurt. More than acceptable, really. Such a feat might be lauded. Joggers have long since ceased to be gawked at. They run, and people, I think, envy them. Two of the people I admire most are elderly walkers, a couple of men who walk briskly each morning through my neighborhood. They are disciplined, active and caring.

Kenny Moore, the noted author and marathoner from Eugene, perhaps said it best: "Running is not some counterculture movement in Eugene, but has been welcomed by the business community and all walks of life." Clearly, it is a lifestyle. After some early publicity, it became forgotten that Les Anderson, then the mayor, ran in marathons, clocked 5:30 in the jogger's mile at age 54, and bicycled to work. He was not considered eccentric, but physically fit.

Admittedly, Eugene is special. Your community may never have a winter without snow, or a summer without prolonged heat and humidity. Your community probably won't have a track team that wins national championships and a stadium which has hosted the last two United States Olympic trials in track and field.

But it doesn't mean your community can't improve its

running environment. I've visited cities where the high school tracks are closed when school is not in session. I, better than anyone, understand what joggers can do to the synthetic track. They have literally worn ours out. But should the track be left simply for the use of a competitive few? Absolutely not.

Eugene, despite its reputation, is not overburdened with good running facilities. There are a number of fine tracks, but most joggers will soon tire of running around a track, if indeed they ever set foot on one in the first place. Most of our joggers run primarily on the streets. And as their numbers increased, a problem developed. Both in congestion and sore legs. It was Steve Prefontaine's fondest hope that Eugene could have a series of jogging trails like those he had admired and enjoyed in Europe. Sadly, it took his death in 1975 to stimulate the building of a beautiful jogging facility we now know as Pre's Trail. If golfers seek out Pebble Beach, tennis addicts Wimbledon and baseball fans Yankee Stadium, then the nation's joggers should all want to set a foot on Pre's Trail.

"It's incredible how many calls we get to our office from people across the nation wanting information on how to duplicate the facility," said Mike Dooley, a man who helped design the trail. There is little question that it is the longest and best facility of its type in the country.

While most trails in Europe measure only 1,000 meters, or less than a mile, Pre's Trail is almost five miles of soft, wood composition trails forming numerous loops through a park along the Willamette River, which cuts through the heart of the city. A runner can be cooled by the canopy of a filbert orchard, or charmed by light dancing off the adjacent river, or baked by the starkness of an open area which was once the city's garbage dump, or rewarded by a grove of tall firs, a three-mile run from the heart of the park. And all at a minimum cost to the legs and backs of the joggers. The trail is a soft alternative to Eugene's streets, sidewalks and bike paths. It is also free of cars and bikes, allowing runners the solitude and safety of their

Pre's Trail is almost five miles of soft, wood-composition trails in a park near the Willamette River and downtown Eugene.

A special spot on Pre's Trail is an old filbert orchard that cools runners in the summer with a leafy canopy.

own facility. Pre's Trail is a unique facility in America, but not one which other communities can regard as impossible to duplicate. Pre's Trail is valued at almost $100,000, although it cost county taxpayers less than $10,000. The area's wood products industry answered the pleas of the Oregon Track Club for hog fuel—byproducts of the lumber industry such as wood waste, cedar shavings, and sawdust—to cover the 10-foot-wide trail. Quickly, industry donated 1,000 units of wood waste at a value of $60,000.

Joggers themselves turned out to help apply much of the soft material on the trails. They also helped cut away blackberry vines and other vegetation which constantly threatens to narrow trails. And, each Labor Day, the Prefontaine Foundation holds its annual Pre's Trail Run, with those who enter receiving a T-shirt donated by the Nike Shoe Company for a $4 donation to the foundation for annual upkeep on the trail. Normally, about 1,000 runners make donations.

Should you consider a Pre's Trail–type facility in your community, you should seek materials indigenous to your area as a covering for the running surface. For many years we used rubber waste on a warmup loop inside the track at Hayward Field. Such a composition could be perfect for those communities in the industrial Northeast. Packed sand might work. Who knows what an ingenious mind and a resourceful community could come up with? Many communities are concerned about saving much of their park area in a relatively wild state. A running path does little to detract from the beauty of the area, and joggers are generally not people to litter and destroy the environment.

In one small area of the park, we added the parcours to Pre's Trail. It consists of six exercise stations spread along an approximate three-fourths of a mile section of the trail which are designed to do for the body what running can't do. Roscoe Divine, the former miler, uses the parcours after one of his five-mile runs. "When I'm done with my run," he says, "I'll jog easily from station to station for my exercises." Pre's Trail parcours has its stations set up in a definite order: the stretch bar platform, a horizontal ladder, a poleclimb, a bar jump, a balance beam and finally parallel bars. At each station, there is a sign depicting how the station should be used. Unlike the traditional European parcours which sets up a program with desired repetitions at each station, the one in Pre's Trail tells you no such thing. "Setting up goals could lead a lot of people astray," said Dr. Stan James, a jogger and

Parcours stations along Pre's Trail such as the stretch bar platform for situps enhance conditioning of the whole body.

orthopedic surgeon, who helped put in the parcours. "It might encourage some people to do more than they should, or others to do less. I personally do other exercises in the gym, but I think for an outdoor exercise area the parcours is quite good. My concept of fitness is all-around fitness and jogging alone won't do it."

The Scandinavian influence, of course, is heavy in Eugene. It prompted Prefontaine to suggest the jogging trail in the first place and was behind the eventual illumination of more than half the trail. Small, smoke-tinted globes 12 feet off the ground are spaced 150 feet apart in open areas and 120 feet apart in the wooded glens.

"I spent a year in Oslo, Norway," said Divine, who is a leading member of the Prefontaine Foundation, "and the city has over 50 ski trails that are lit at night. A father can come home from work, have dinner and then take the family out for five or six miles of skiing. I'm convinced that this contributed a lot to the physical and mental health of the citizens of Oslo."

There was a genuine and understandable concern that lights would destroy the tranquility of Pre's Trail. "We weren't interested in great big lights on high poles," said landscape designer Mike Dooley. "We kept the quiet, secluded atmosphere of the trail, yet give joggers another two or three hours to run after dark." Darkness comes early during our Northwest winters, and those who use the trail as a conditioner for skiing have benefited greatly. The parcours, of course, is part of the lighted section. Lights are turned on at dusk by a photo cell and turned off by a pre-set switch at 9 P.M.

Pre's Trail acts as headquarters for Eugene's jogging community, which long ago disdained the tough, competitive runs for what the Oregon Track Club calls its "fun runs." At least once a month the club holds a run beginning at Pre's Trail. The distances are two and four miles. Some runners go both distances; some race one and jog the other. Some jog slowly as groups, talking all the way and refusing to race one another. Some really go at it. A potluck dinner can flavor the affair; so can other gimmick events. One new year was brought in with a race at Pre's Trail which began late one year and ended at about 1 A.M. the next year. A local restaurant sponsors a relay race in which one member of the team runs six miles, another canoes down our Willamette River and a third cycles the remaining distance. Our summer all-comers meets at Hayward Field on the University of Oregon campus feature the jogger's mile, where winning is based on running

The environment is not just facilities but people, like this mother and daughter running easily on a trail.

as close to a predicted time as possible. Pace, not speed, becomes the runner's passion.

Too much cannot be made of the Oregon Track Club's influence on Eugene's jogging environment. The club is both strong enough and diverse enough to stage the United States Olympic Trials for track and field and a series of five all-comers meets in the same summer. The club helps world-class track athletes travel across the globe in search of competition, and also puts on the monthly fun runs at Pre's Trail. Obviously, its support and influence are broad-based. A strong, well-rounded track club is important to your community.

It will evolve, of course, that your running community will have its two or three major competitive events each year. The big events take care of themselves. They are celebrated, publicized and generally well attended. It is the fun runs, the potluck, the every-morning-running-groups, however, that make for a good jogging environment. Those activities make the big ones possible. And the little ones go on forever.

10

Eugene's Joggers

Sally Smith

Sally is the 43-year-old mother of two sons, ages 18 and 14. She works at the University of Oregon as a director of student housing. She and her husband Ev have run for 11 years. Sally likes people and makes running a social event. She never runs alone; in fact, she starts the day off running through her neighborhood with her husband and their malamute Kahiva. She occasionally runs with co-workers during the lunch hour, and she and her husband plan weekend outings with friends that center around a long, relaxed run. "We even look forward to running on our vacations," she says. "I've run around Temple Square in Salt Lake City, across the Golden Gate Bridge in San Francisco, and through an awful lot of very pretty city parks that most people don't take the time to even see." Sally started running before her husband did. She was prompted by her babysitter, a star on the local high school track team. "One morning I just got up and decided to run around the block. We were from the Midwest and had never heard of jogging, but since we lived so close to the

Sally and Ev Smith and their malamute, Kahiva, take off on their morning three-mile run, just as they've been doing for ten years.

university we became aware of track. The first month or so I tried to get a neighbor to go with me, but after the first week she was never there. Ev started running several months later. We'd get up every morning at 6:30, wake up the kids, turn on the coffee pot, and by the time we'd get back the kids would be up and the coffee would be starting its first perk." Why does Sally jog? "I'd never been very talkative in the mornings," she explained. "In fact, they called me Silent Sal. I just wasn't very agreeable. But after I got into the habit of running every morning, I felt so rather noble about what I was doing it just wasn't worth getting mad about things anymore. I had put myself together for the day. I never liked getting up in the morning, but now I get up to run. I just don't miss my run, and if I do I feel sorry for myself all day. When I'm running I don't need much sleep and I don't get very hungry." For years, Sally ran one mile each morning. Five years ago all of that changed. "I had to go to a meeting in Springfield," she said, "and I decided I would jog over there. It was perfectly easy, I had no trouble running three miles. I found I could run longer and longer and it didn't bother me a bit. Now I run between three and five miles a day, and we usually go for a longer run on the weekends. I've run up to 9 miles, but that takes a big chunk of time out of your day. On the weekends we will get together with friends and plan a run that will take us back to our house for coffee and doughnuts. Or go on a route that will take us to a restaurant. I don't know why for sure, but the people I like best also like to run." Sally talks about the enjoyment of running with someone. "The rhythm of running with someone is almost like dancing," she says. "It is a physically pleasant sensation to be in contact with a running partner. Later, we compare notes. I know if Ev wanted to be mean to me, he could say he wasn't going to run with me." Sally has run in summer all-comers track meets and with the help of some friends broke eight minutes in the mile. "I ran 7:58 two years ago, that's about my pace. I seem to run that fast whether I'm running one mile or four miles. I was timed at four miles once and ran 32 minutes and 30 seconds." Sally looked ahead. "Sometimes I wonder what I'll look like when I'm 63 and still running." Chances are she'll find out.

Bill Lynch

Bill is a 57-year-old newspaper reporter for the *Eugene Register-Guard.* "I never tell anybody that running will

Bill Lynch, 57 years old, jogs to extend his middle age.

prevent a heart attack," says Bill Lynch, "but I strongly believe—and the doctors supported my contention—that it does reduce the damage done by the heart attack." Bill Lynch had jogged religiously for almost 15 years when he suffered a heart attack on November 16, 1973. People were stunned that it could happen to Bill. Six months later, Bill ran two miles in 16:30. The next month he climbed 11,000-foot Mt. Hood. "I was thinking the other day about running track in high school. I was a miler at a small school in Wisconsin. The school we were running against didn't have a miler, so my coach ran me in an exhibition two-mile. He was criticized for letting an 18-year-old overdo. Forty years later, and forty years older, nobody says anything about me going on a seven-mile run." Although

Bill Lynch continues to run his three miles each afternoon after work, he does not run for the love of running. "It's basic to other things that I do. I run so I can be a downhill skier, so I can be a mountain climber, so I can play touch football. I believe running has extended my middle age," continued Bill. "I ski as steep a slope as my children and nephews and nieces. They are in their twenties and I can be just as foolish as they are. I lead them on mountain climbs each year and am really able to enjoy them. So many of my friends and relatives are at the end of their middle age and they are 10 years younger than me." Bill ran in high school but didn't do any more running until he was about 35 years old and first took up an interest in mountain climbing and skiing. "I'd go on a three-week running program each spring to get in shape for climbing. It worked fine for a while, but as I got older it hurt so much to get in shape that it was taking me more like six weeks to get in shape. I decided at that time—which was just about the time Bill Bowerman got back from New Zealand and started talking about year-around running—that I was going to have to run all year or give up climbing and skiing." When the heart attack hit, Bill wondered if he'd ever run, climb, or ski again. "I believe I had a strong heart muscle when the attack came," he said, "and one doctor told me I had 2½-times the normal amount of capillaries in the heart to help supply blood to the damaged area. I was afraid that I might become a heart cripple, that people would think I was less capable than before. I made up my mind that if it was possible I would be back running and climbing. The doctors really held me back. I started with a walking program, and I have to admit I was so conscious of my heart beat. But after awhile I wanted to jog, and finally demanded that they let me jog. I took a stress test and they said I was okayed to jog. Six months after my heart attack I ran two miles and that cleared me in my mind to climb Mt. Hood in June." Bill says he feels stronger than ever. He runs three miles a day, four days a week. "I run an occasional six or seven mile road run to celebrate and get a T-shirt. I used to play touch football instead, but I didn't quit playing, the team did." Bill had a final word of advice: "It's not the running you do after a heart attack that helps you but rather the strength you build up before."

Ed Swartz

Ed Swartz is not your typical jogger. "Put me on the cover of your book, a cigarette in one hand and a drink in the other and I'll draw some new readers," he says. Ed laughs about his image as a jogger. "I violate all the rules. I'm 35 pounds overweight, I smoke (half-pack a day), I drink, and I've had a knee operated on three times. And yet," he continued, "I haven't missed more than a week away from running in seven years." Unlike those who run for the sake of physical fitness and appearance, Ed Swartz, 43, runs for the mental therapy three miles and 30 minutes each morning can offer him. All of Ed's life has been centered around athletics. He was a football player and wrestler at Iowa State Teachers College. And then a coach of both of those sports. Then, in 1970, came a job change away from coaching and into administration. To dealing with people. To stress. "I began waking up early in the morning," he said. "It's called insomnia, except I didn't have insomnia because I got up. I was up, I thought my dog needed exercise, so I began to run. It started out with a mile, and I thought a mile was the end of the world. Now it's a steady three miles a day. I've gone as far as seven miles, but I've never gone the real gung-ho stuff and I don't ever want to run under the stress of time or competition." Although he feels that he is 35 pounds overweight (Ed is 5 foot 6 and weighs 205 pounds), Ed says he doesn't run to lose weight. Or to prepare himself for any other physical activity. "Running became therapy for me," he said. "When you are an aggressive person and tend to go after people you must deal with, you need time to think through how you're going to deal with people. I go one-on-one with myself for 30 minutes each day. I can really understand

Ed Swartz likes to exercise, would like to play more racquetball, but finds the only thing he can depend on is his morning run.

these people who meditate; I seem to get the same benefit and exercise too. I am often in a trance over those three miles. But I get answers to my problems. I never push it." Ed runs alone. He's avoided suggestions of others to form an early morning jogging group. It's his time to be alone, and to think. "I like running in the morning," he says. "I'm not the same guy running at noon that I am in the morning. I run my three miles on the golf course right outside our home. I hate the track; it's drudgery." Ed has a favorite saying about his jogging. "You can't take that away from me," he'll say when anyone asks why he runs each morning. "During the course of a day," he explains, "I'll have a thousand things I'm not going to get done. I'll say I'm going to have an afternoon workout. But, here I am paying $25 to a racquetball club each month, and I can't even get it going enough to establish three people to play with. That's ridiculous, and I know it is. So when I've run in the morning, no matter what else happens, that's one in the bag. I've done it, and maybe I can't do anything else that day, or maybe I go off and drink too much, or eat too much, or smoke too much, no matter what I do, I've had my morning run and they can't take that away from me."

Les Anderson

Les Anderson is not your ordinary jogger, either. His son, Jon, made the 1972 Olympic team in the 10,000 meters and won the 1973 Boston Marathon, but, in many respects, Les is more remarkable than Jon. After all, he began running before his son took it up. "I was a personal friend of Bill Bowerman's," said Les, "and I got interested in running when he got back from New Zealand. I was getting fat. I remember a picture my wife took of me on a sailboat when I was 41 years old. I weighed 190 pounds then, my ski pants were getting tighter; it was time to do something." Les Anderson is now 56 years old. And weighs 170 pounds. And looks 46. Two years ago Les ran a 26-mile marathon in 3:38. "I plan to run another one, one of these days," he says. Last year, Les ran a personal record 5:32 in the jogger's mile during our summer all-comers track meets. Of course, much of Les's fame comes from his eight-year tenure as Eugene's mayor. He ruled the city during the 1972 and 1976 Olympic Trials at the University of Oregon, and during the period when Steve Prefontaine rose to national stature and jogging replaced rain as the No. 1 topic of conversation. "I enjoyed being identified with the jogging community," he said, "and if I gave jogging a boost by being a running mayor then so much

Les Anderson may be Eugene's most famous jogger: eight years' mayor, father of Boston Marathon winner Jon, and marathon finisher himself at age 54. (Photo courtesy of Les Anderson)

the better." Les, at age 56, runs 25 miles a week. He runs in the morning, about 6:30, and covers between three to six miles a day, four times a week with a longer run—7 or 8 miles—on the weekend. "It's the discipline involved in running that ties so many things together," Les explains. "You can't smoke heavily and jog, you can't be heavy and jog, and you have to get quite a bit of rest and eat reasonably well to jog." A year ago, Les and another Eugene jogger—Les was 55 years old and his friend was 54—joined a party of 12 in a 30-day mountain climbing expedition to Nepal where they climbed 21,000-foot Mt. Mera. "I can honestly say," said Anderson, "that we were in the best shape of anybody in the party, and we were by far the oldest." Les has been jogging for 17 years. What tips might he have for would-be joggers? "No. 1, have good equipment, including shoes that are a pleasure to put on. Wear clean, dry clothing that will protect you from the elements. No. 2, find a pleasant place to run. Whirling around a track is like doing so many pushups. When I was mayor and we had zoning problems, or street-paving problems coming up on the agenda, I used to include those sites in my jogging route. No. 3, get your mind ready for a long run. Before I go out I think of a couple of things I might want to think about on the run. Do anything you can to get your mind off the putting of one foot in front of the other. Personally, I look forward to a certain exhilaration when I run—and generally find it."

Jim Ferguson

It was only slightly more than a year ago that Jim Ferguson reached that point of no return. "I felt that I was sluggish," he said, "and I saw no reason for a 39-year-old to be that out of shape. I realized that my cardiovascular system was not in the shape it should be." So Jim Ferguson, the golf coach and physical education instructor at the University of Oregon, began to jog. He tried a few times before, lasted two or three months, got discouraged, and quit. The immediate goal a year ago was to run in a fund-raising jog-a-thon for the golf team. He wanted to be able to run as far as his golfers in the one-hour period. "After that," he said, "I thought if I could run for 15 or 20 minutes at a time, then why couldn't I run longer? So I slowly increased the time and distance of my jogs. After eight months I was up to an hour a day and I've been there ever since." Jim is pretty pleased with what's happened to him during the last year of jogging. "I feel so much better than before, and the better I felt the more I wanted to run. During that first year of jogging and some dieting, I lost 25 pounds, and my heart beat at rest dropped from 76 to 60." But as it happens to most joggers, Jim Ferguson, too, began to appreciate the mental benefits

Jim Ferguson saw no reason why a 39-year-old should be sluggish and out of shape, so he started jogging.

of jogging as much, if not more, than the physical ones. "I'm kind of a solitary person," he explained. "I like to think I spend time on my run in prayer. Actually, I do pray a lot while I'm running. I talk to myself, and think about what I've done during the day and what I need to accomplish the next day." Ferguson feels a lessening of tensions because of his running program. "I believe a lot of men and women in jobs with a high degree of tension would benefit from jogging; it's a time to release that tension. I know my time with my family is more meaningful now because I'm thinking less about my job and what I did that day after my run is over in the evening. And I'm feeling good; I've just had a hot shower. And, too, I have a tendency to eat less at dinner, which is good for me." Ferguson, an athlete in high school and college, obviously has a big appetite for running. He says the hour a day hasn't drained him, or left him susceptible to injury. "I had one cold for two or three days during the year," he said, "I've just really felt good." Jim runs two or three different loops through his neighborhood. "I just decided jogging would be a part of my lifestyle. I organize my life daily, and 5 to 6 in the afternoon I will jog, just like I get up at 6:30 and I eat from noon to 12:30. It happens regardless of the situation. Maybe I miss once every two or three weeks." Jim runs with his big dog and finds that the two inadvertently are involved in some Fartlek training. "He likes to run fast, so periodically we'll just pick up the pace. I've never had an injury jogging, although I have to admit that it always hurts a little when I'm running. I mean I never get through two or three miles and think I just feel super. I guess that's just the way it is." Although Jim is obviously in shape to run in some type of road run, he says he'll stay away from competition. "I don't think I'd like running with a lot of people," he says. "I'd just rather be by myself."

Lloyd Staples

When Lloyd Staples says there are two obvious benefits from jogging—physical and mental—and can't decide which is the most important, that's saying something. Lloyd Staples is 70 years old, an emeritus professor of geology at the University of Oregon, a jogger as long as he can remember, and survivor of a heart attack. "Nobody believed I would be a heart attack-type victim," he says. "I'm not overweight—never have been—I don't smoke, and I've always been physically active. I've done all the things you're supposed to do. But, it's just like the plumbing in an old house, I guess. Sometimes it gets plugged up. Apparently all that I had was an area of one of the major arteries that plugged very rapidly. Well, I went to the hospital, they fixed it with a bypass, and in just a short

At age 66, Lloyd Staples survived open heart surgery and four months later was back jogging. He started jogging before it was fashionable.

time I was back on the track again." Lloyd was 66 when he went through open heart surgery. "There aren't too many people my age who go through surgery and start jogging again. I really think my ability to survive the attack so readily and come back so fast was because I was in good physical shape." Lloyd was jogging one day when he said he felt a heaviness in his throat. The pain continued to build until four days later he could barely get from his car to the office without help. "I had lots of warning and was able to get to the hospital in time," he says, "and I'm not sure you have that kind of warning and that kind of time without being in good shape." Long before jogging was really popular, and even before Bill Bowerman came back from New Zealand spreading its gospel, Lloyd Staples was running. "A geology professor when I was doing my undergraduate work at Columbia told me what it took to be a geologist: You have to have brains, the ability to stick it out, and like the outdoors. A geologist is half legs. Being able to scamper up and down hills is of great benefit." For more than 20 years, Lloyd ran around the intramural track behind Hayward Field. Two miles a day, nothing more, nothing less. "Oh, on Sundays, I might go over to the community college and run on their cross-country course for my two miles. But," he continued, "I picked two miles because it was the optimum time for me. For years I had my jogging scheduled as if it were a class. That way, I wasn't interrupted. I think this is what you have to do if you're going to be regular. Two miles was all I really had time for. In the hour I had scheduled I had to get to the gym, get my running clothes on, run, take a shower and get back to my next class." Two miles around the same track for 20 years could get a little boring. It could, but didn't for Lloyd Staples. "There is something about jogging—when you aren't pushing yourself too hard—which is extremely relaxing. People would think that you have a tendency to review all of your problems while you run, but I know I tend to just turn them off and let my mind wander—it's sort of a halfway point between being awake and asleep. You kind of just drift and dream as you run. You think of things, you plan your next vacation, but nothing very serious because you realize you're not supposed to be working at the time."

Dick and Kelly Wicklund

Dick is 38 years old and a Eugene pediatrician. His wife, Kelly, is 36, mother of three sons, and a former

Dick and Kelly Wicklund compete annually in the Physicians' Mile and have run the Bay-to-Breakers in San Francisco.

championship speed skater in Minnesota. The Wicklunds like the outdoors; they ski, play tennis, and run. Although neither will come right out and say it, they are both very competitive. "We hadn't thought about running, until one summer—it was 1972—we decided to run in the medical association's annual joggers' mile. We ran a mile the week before just to see if we could do it," explained Dick. "It was a night after some spaghetti and a couple of glasses of wine that we ran. It was in some old tennis shoes, I'm sure, and I ran a 7:10 and my wife a 7:25. I guess I ran because I had to beat her." That started it. Dick began running almost every morning with a group of other physicians, and Kelly joined a bigger group which made five-mile jaunts each Saturday morning. "We go a nice casual three miles in the morning," continued Dick, "it's more the fellowship than some kind of exercise thing for us. We chat about ski conditions, basketball, and what's going on in the medical community. We consider ourselves the gentlemen joggers—it's never a race, never a pushy-type thing." Kelly runs far less regularly than Dick. She normally runs with Dick in the Saturday morning group, but doesn't have the every-other-morning runs. "I run pretty much when I feel like it," she says. "I run at a pace that feels comfortable and I normally feel quite invigorated." Kelly is bothered by occasional back and knee problems, so as far as she is concerned too little running is better than too much. Both Dick and Kelly enjoy the Saturday morning group which includes other doctors and their wives and other good friends. "We usually have a nice conversation going," said Kelly. "I like the social aspect; I like the people we're around." The fun runs provide a good social backdrop for the Wicklunds and keep them in shape for tennis and skiing. But there is the competitive side to both of them which doesn't go unnoticed. Kelly has turned in the fastest mile time of any of the doctor's wives—she ran 6:06 two years ago—and Dick trains for the medical society five-mile run. "I like to keep track of my times," says Dick. "I compete off a training base acquired from jogging, but it's fun to see how you stack up against others, and how your times have improved." Dick's mile time dropped from 7:10 that first time to 6:20 the next year to 5:40 in 1977. But the minute you type Dick as highly competitive, then he talks about his Thursday run—or the relaxing time he has on his day off. "If I can squeeze in a run, I might go five to seven miles," he says. "I really like running by myself. I just put my mind in neutral; I might think about something, and then again I might not. Chances are I won't remember if I was thinking or not." Once in a while, Dick will take one or all of his sons on the Thursday run. "The kids get their bikes, we go five miles or more and we chat along the way. I think that's kind of nice." Dick thought for a moment about 6:30 A.M. and his run the next morning with the other doctors. "I'm not a guy who likes to get up in the morning," he said, "but I find if I roll over, pretty soon the kids are going out the door to school, and I'm late getting to the hospital. When I jog I get places on time. Jogging gets me off on the right foot."

About the Authors

Bill Dellinger has been the coach of the University of Oregon track team since 1973 when he succeeded his coach, Bill Bowerman. Dellinger competed in three Olympic Games for the United States, won a bronze medal in the 1964 Games at Tokyo, and at one time held American records in the 1,500 meters, the two-mile, the three-mile and the 5,000 meters. He began coaching Oregon's cross-country team even before taking over as track coach and his distance runners have won four of the last seven national cross-country championships. Dellinger concluded competitive running in 1964 and has jogged regularly for the past 13 years. He was Steve Prefontaine's personal coach and believes the program Prefontaine used to set every American distance record can be adapted to you.

Blaine Newnham is the sports editor of the *Eugene Register-Guard* and recognized as one of the country's top writers of track and field. He has had articles published in many national magazines, including *Sports Illustrated.* Newnham moved his family to Eugene in 1971 after covering the Oakland Raiders of the National Football League and the San Francisco Giants of the National League for the *Oakland Tribune.* Newnham was voted Oregon's sports writer of the year in 1974, his investigative story on the closure of Crater Lake National Park won several national awards, and in 1976 the *Eugene Register-Guard* was judged to have the best sports page of any newspaper in the country. Newnham is a daily jogger.

Warren Morgan is a photographer for the *Eugene Register-Guard* and an addicted runner. A graduate of the United States Naval Academy, Morgan taught school before joining the *Register-Guard* as a photographer in 1975. He has since become a runner and in 1977 ran his first marathon. Later that same year, in Portland, Oregon, Morgan ran a second marathon, broke the three-hour barrier, and qualified for the Boston Marathon. Morgan both understands and photographs runners.

Bill Dellinger

Blaine Newnham

Warren Morgan

Index

C

D

E